FOUNDATION *Accounting*

workbook

NVQ LEVEL 2
ACCOUNTING

David Cox
Michael Fardon

Published by Osborne Books Limited
Unit 1B Everoak Estate
Bromyard Road
Worcester WR2 5HN
Tel 01905 748071
Email books@osbornebooks.co.uk
Website www.osbornebooks.co.uk

Cover and page design by Hedgehog

Printed by the Bath Press, Bath

British Library Cataloguing in Publication Data
A catalogue record for this book is available from the British Library

ISBN 1 872962 24 6

CONTENTS

practice Simulations

practice Central Assessments

ACKNOWLEDGEMENTS

The authors wish to thank the following for their help with the compilation, reading and production of this workbook: Jean Cox, Jon Moore and Roger Petheram. Special thanks are due to Janet Brammer for providing the Workbook Activities for Unit 4.

Thanks are also due to the Association of Accounting Technicians for their generous permission in allowing the reproduction of the sample Central Assessment 'Paperstop' and to the Inland Revenue for the provision of form P30B, which is Crown Copyright and reproduced here with the permission of Her Majesty's Stationery Office.

HOW TO USE THIS BOOK

Foundation Accounting Workbook is designed to be used alongside the Osborne Books' *Foundation Accounting Tutorial* and is ideal for student use in the classroom, at home and on distance learning courses.

Foundation Accounting Workbook is divided into three separate sections: workbook activities, practice Simulations and practice Central Assessments.

The Simulations and Central Assessment tasks in this workbook provide, within the text, the documents and accounts that need to be completed. In the case of the Workbook Activities, most documents are provided in the text, but some formats, eg double-entry accounts, journals, cash books, are not. They are reproduced in the Appendix at the end of the book, and may be photocopied. Financial documents are also available for download from the Resources section of the Osborne Books website: www.osbornebooks.co.uk

workbook activities

Workbook activities are self-contained exercises which are designed to supplement the activities in the tutorial text. Many of them are more extended than the exercises in *Foundation Accounting Tutorial* and provide useful practice for students preparing for Assessments.

practice Simulations

There is a set of tasks for each of the NCVQ units. These have been newly written for Osborne Books and are designed to cover the performance criteria of each Unit.

practice Central Assessments

The first of these is newly written for Osborne Books and is based on the format of the second which has kindly been provided by AAT.

answers

Answers are not provided in the text. A Tutor Pack is available separately. Please telephone Osborne Books on 01905 748071 for details.

David Cox
Michael Fardon

Summer 2000

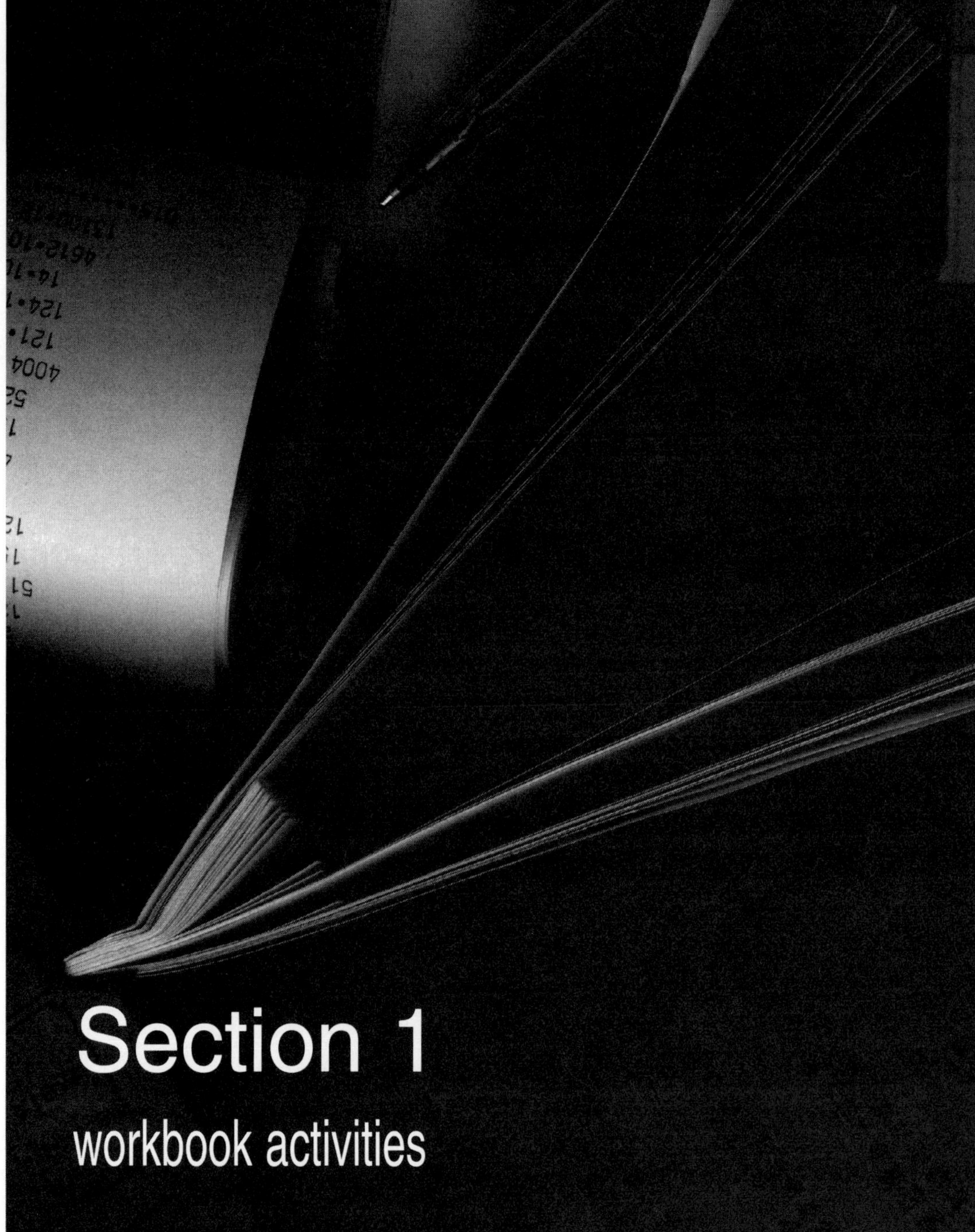

Section 1

workbook activities

This section contains activities which are suitable for use with the individual chapters of 'Foundation Accounting Tutorial' from Osborne Books.

Activities have not been included for Chapters 14 and 15. This is because they are supplementary 'background' chapters on the subjects of Communication and Law.

1 INTRODUCTION TO ACCOUNTING

1.1 What is the difference between a sole trader, a partnership and a limited company in terms of the following factors?

- ownership of the business
- the ability to specialise in one area of the business
- liability for business debts
- the need to keep accounting records

Set out your answer in the form of a table with the above factors as headings.

1.2 Give three examples of revenue expenditure and three examples of capital expenditure.

1.3 The accounting records of Tom's sole trader business show the following account totals at the end of the year:

Capital (money invested by the owner)	£185,000
Business premises	£100,000
Bank overdraft (owed to the bank)	£80,000
Computers used in the business	£50,000
Stock held by the business	£75,000
Creditors (amounts owed by the business)	£20,000
Debtors (money owed to the business)	£60,000

(a) Sort the above accounts under the three categories set out below, and total each category:

- assets
- liabilities
- capital

(b) Insert the three totals into the accounting equation

assets minus liabilities equals capital

If the equation does not balance, check your categories in (a) above.

(c) Tom has increased the bank overdraft to buy more stock costing £10,000. Adjust the totals in the equation. It should still balance; if it does not, check your workings.

2 DOCUMENTS FOR GOODS AND SERVICES SUPPLIED

INTRODUCTION

You work as an accounts assistant at Compusupply Limited, a business which sells computer supplies such as disks and listing paper to a wide range of customers.

It is your job to process incoming orders which arrive in the form of purchase orders, faxes and telephoned orders.

You also deal with the accounting side of returned goods and you issue credit notes when credit is due.

You are also in charge of sending out statements.

You are authorised to issue invoices without reference to the accounts supervisor as long as the account is kept within its credit limit. You are required to refer any difficulties and likely excesses over credit limits to your supervisor.

Compusupply Limited normally operates a computer accounting system, but unfortunately the system has crashed and you have been asked to process all the necessary documents by hand until the hard disk has been repaired. The crash is a serious one, so you may be without the computer for over a week.

You have been given the following information:

CUSTOMER DETAILS
(EXTRACTS FROM COMPUSUPPLY FILES)

customer	account number	discount %	credit limit £	balance £
Andrews R C	234	10	1000	750.00
Harber Employment Agency	341	10	1000	456.75
Case, Justin	209	10	1000	218.50
P C Mack Limited	197	20	5000	3190.00
Singh, I	222	10	1000	00.00
Singh, R, Retail	265	20	3500	2185.00
Townsend Litho	409	20	5000	4756.75
Zebra Designs Ltd	376	10	1000	487.50

COMPUSUPPLY CATALOGUE (EXTRACT)

code	product	unit price	£ (excl VAT)
OMHD10	OM 3.5 inch diskettes DSHD	boxes of 10	5.50
Z100	Zip 100MB cartridges	each	12.99
LP80	Computer listing paper 80 column	2000 sheet box	14.99
LP132	Computer listing paper 132 column	2000 sheet box	19.99
SQ44	Syquest disk 44MB	each	36.99
SQ88	Syquest disk 88MB	each	42.99
SQ200	Syquest disk 200MB	each	49.99
DB40	Floppy storage box (40 disks)	each	4.99
DB80	Floppy storage box (80 disks)	each	5.99
AG1	VDU anti-glare screen (mesh)	each	11.99
AG2	VDU anti-glare screen (glass)	each	19.99

ACTIVITIES

2.1 You have to check a batch of invoices to make sure the correct customer trade discount of 10% has been applied.

The totals before deduction of discount are:

(a) £67.50

(b) £45.00

(c) £107.95

(d) £12,567.95

(e) £12.75

(f) £89.00

(g) £400.00

(h) £17,450.50

(i) £1.75

(j) £30.33

You are to work out the net totals before VAT. Remember to round up or down to nearest penny.

2.2 You have to check the VAT calculation on a further batch of invoices. The totals before VAT are:

(a) £40.00

(b) £8.00

(c) £75.00

(d) £675.50

You are to work out the VAT *and* the final total in each case. Remember to round VAT amounts down to the nearest penny in each case.

2.3 Your colleague reminds you that a cash discount of 2.5% is due on the four invoices in the previous task. You are to adjust the VAT to allow for a cash discount of 2.5% and recalculate the totals, but remembering that the net total shown on the invoice will *not* be reduced - only the VAT amount.

2.4 In the morning post there are three purchase orders. You are to complete invoices for all three orders. The date is 20 October 2001 and the invoices should be numbered consecutively from 309530. Blank invoices are printed on the pages that follow the purchase orders.

JUSTIN CASE ***insurance services***
2 Oakfield Business Centre
Letchfield
LT1 7TR
Tel 01903 273423

PURCHASE ORDER

TO

Compusupply Limited
Unit 17 Elgar Estate,
Broadfield, BR7 4ER

purchase order no 58345

date 17 October 2001

product code	quantity	description
LP80	2 boxes	Computer listing paper, 80 columns

Authorised signature *J Case* date *17.10.01*

R SINGH RETAIL
2 The Crescent
Broadfield
BR6 3TR
Tel 01908 456291

PURCHASE ORDER

TO
Compusupply Limited
Unit 17 Elgar Estate,
Broadfield, BR7 4ER

purchase order no 353453

date 17 October 2001

product code	quantity	description
OMHD10	10	OM 3.5 inch floppy disks

Authorised signature *R Singh* date *17.10.01*

P C Mack Ltd
57 New Road
Broadfield
BR3 6TF
Tel 01908 456291

PURCHASE ORDER

TO
Compusupply Limited
Unit 17 Elgar Estate,
Broadfield, BR7 4ER

purchase order no 14535

date 15 October 2001

product code	quantity	description
SQ44	2	Syquest 44MB disks

Authorised signature *Steve Gates* date *15.10.01*

INVOICE

COMPUSUPPLY LIMITED

Unit 17 Elgar Estate, Broadfield, BR7 4ER
Tel 01908 765756 Fax 01908 765777 Email rob@compusupply.u-net.com
VAT Reg GB 0745 4689 13

invoice to

invoice no

account

your reference

date/tax point

product code	description	quantity	price	unit	total	discount %	net

goods total	
VAT	
TOTAL	

terms
Net monthly
Carriage paid
E & OE

INVOICE

COMPUSUPPLY LIMITED

Unit 17 Elgar Estate, Broadfield, BR7 4ER
Tel 01908 765756 Fax 01908 765777 Email rob@compusupply.u-net.com
VAT Reg GB 0745 4689 13

invoice to

invoice no

account

your reference

date/tax point

product code	description	quantity	price	unit	total	discount %	net

goods total	
VAT	
TOTAL	

terms
Net monthly
Carriage paid
E & OE

INVOICE

COMPUSUPPLY LIMITED

Unit 17 Elgar Estate, Broadfield, BR7 4ER
Tel 01908 765756 Fax 01908 765777 Email rob@compusupply.u-net.com
VAT Reg GB 0745 4689 13

invoice to

invoice no

account

your reference

date/tax point

product code	description	quantity	price	unit	total	discount %	net
						goods total	
						VAT	
						TOTAL	

terms
Net monthly
Carriage paid
E & OE

2.5 Check the invoice extracts shown below with the Catalogue and customer discount list, making sure that the details and the calculations are correct. Where there are errors, correct them in red ink.

Note: VAT is always rounded down to the nearest penny. No cash discounts are involved.

(a) Invoice to R C Andrews

code	description	quantity	price	total	discount %	net
AG1	VDU anti-glare screen (glass)	1	19.99	19.99	20	15.99
					goods total	15.99
					VAT @ 17.5%	2.79
					TOTAL	18.78

(b) Invoice to I Singh

code	description	quantity	price	total	discount %	net
DB40	Floppy storage box (40)	4	4.99	19.96	10	15.97

goods total	15.97
VAT @ 17.5%	2.79
TOTAL	13.18

(c) Invoice to Harber Employment Agency

code	description	quantity	price	total	discount %	net
OMHD10	OM 3.5 inch disks DSHD	10 boxes	5.50	55.00	20	44.00

goods total	44.00
VAT @ 17.5%	7.70
TOTAL	51.70

2.6 When you return from lunch there are two telephone messages for you:

> **telephone message**
>
> **to** *order processing*
>
> **date** *20.10.01* **time** *13.45*
>
> *Townsend Litho telephoned. They want to order ten 200MB Syquest disks as soon as possible. Can you get them off by carrier today? Thanks. Sue.*

Townsend Litho is a well-established customer with a good record of paying on time.

> **telephone message**
>
> **to** *order processing*
>
> **date** *20.10.01* **time** *13.45*
>
> *Zebra Designs called. They want a box of computer listing paper. 80 columns.*
>
> *Thanks. Hanif.*

On your return from lunch a colleague mentions that he thought he saw a notice in the local paper about Zebra Designs going 'bust'. You look in the official announcement column of the paper and see that your colleague is correct – a creditors' meeting is called for next Monday. Zebra Designs is in deep financial trouble.

You are to

(a) State what you would do in response to the two telephone messages.

(b) State the likely outcome of the two situations.

2.7 It is now a week later – 27 October 2001 – and the computer system is still not working, so you have to complete all documents by hand.

During the course of the day you receive two returns notes (printed on the next page)

You are to

(a) Write down on the R Singh Retail returns note what has gone wrong with the order.

(b) Complete the credit notes as requested (the documents are printed on the page following the returns notes).

R SINGH RETAIL
2 The Crescent
Broadfield
BR6 3TR
Tel 01908 456291

RETURNS NOTE

TO

Compusupply Limited
Unit 17 Elgar Estate,
Broadfield, BR7 4ER

returns note no 353453

date 22 October 2001

product code	quantity	description
OMHD10	9 boxes	OM 3.5 inch floppy disks

REASON FOR RETURN: too many disks sent - only 10 disks ordered. Please credit.

signature *R Singh* date 22.10.01

P C Mack Ltd
57 New Road
Broadfield
BR3 6TF
Tel 01908 456291

RETURNS NOTE

TO

Compusupply Limited
Unit 17 Elgar Estate,
Broadfield, BR7 4ER

purchase order no 14535

date 23 October 2001

product code	quantity	description
SQ44	1	Syquest 44MB data disk.

REASON FOR RETURN: faulty disk. Please credit.

signature *Steve Gates* date 23.10.01

CREDIT NOTE

COMPUSUPPLY LIMITED

Unit 17 Elgar Estate, Broadfield, BR7 4ER
Tel 01908 765756 Fax 01908 765777 Email rob@compusupply.u-net.com
VAT Reg GB 0745 4689 13

to

credit note no
account
your reference
our invoice
date/tax point

product code	description	quantity	price	unit	total	discount %	net

goods total	
VAT	
TOTAL	

REASON FOR CREDIT:

CREDIT NOTE

COMPUSUPPLY LIMITED

Unit 17 Elgar Estate, Broadfield, BR7 4ER
Tel 01908 765756 Fax 01908 765777 Email rob@compusupply.u-net.com
VAT Reg GB 0745 4689 13

to

credit note no
account
your reference
our invoice
date/tax point

product code	description	quantity	price	unit	total	discount %	net

goods total	
VAT	
TOTAL	

REASON FOR CREDIT:

2.8 It is now 31 October. The computer accounts package has been fixed and will start operating again from Monday 3 November. In the meantime you have to make out the customer statements. Using the start-of-month balances and all the transactions during the month, complete statements for R Singh Retail, P C Mack Limited and Justin Case. The statements are printed in the text.

The two payments you have received for these customers is a cheque for £218.50 from Justin Case on October 7 and a cheque for £3190.00 from P C Mack Limited on October 10.

STATEMENT

COMPUSUPPLY LIMITED

Unit 17 Elgar Estate, Broadfield, BR7 4ER
Tel 01908 765756 Fax 01908 765777 Email rob@compusupply.u-net.com
VAT Reg GB 0745 4689 13

to

account

date

date	details	debit	credit	balance

AMOUNT NOW DUE	

STATEMENT

COMPUSUPPLY LIMITED

Unit 17 Elgar Estate, Broadfield, BR7 4ER
Tel 01908 765756 Fax 01908 765777 Email rob@compusupply.u-net.com
VAT Reg GB 0745 4689 13

to

account

date

date	details	debit	credit	balance

AMOUNT NOW DUE	

STATEMENT

COMPUSUPPLY LIMITED

Unit 17 Elgar Estate, Broadfield, BR7 4ER
Tel 01908 765756 Fax 01908 765777 Email rob@compusupply.u-net.com
VAT Reg GB 0745 4689 13

to

account

date

date	details	debit	credit	balance

AMOUNT NOW DUE	

3 ACCOUNTING FOR CREDIT SALES AND SALES RETURNS

3.1 Which one of the following is a prime document?

(a) sales day book

(b) statement of account sent to T Smith, a debtor

(c) sales invoice

(d) sales account

Answer (a) or (b) or (c) or (d)

3.2 Which one of the following is entered in the sales returns day book?

(a) sales invoice

(b) pro-forma invoice

(c) statement of account sent to T Smith, a debtor

(d) credit note issued

Answer (a) or (b) or (c) or (d)

3.3 Define the following:

- prime document
- primary accounting record
- double-entry book-keeping
- account
- ledger

In the activities which follow, the rate of Value Added Tax is to be calculated at the current rate (17.5% at the time of writing). When calculating VAT amounts, you should ignore fractions of a penny, ie round down to a whole penny.

For Activities 3.4 and 3.5 use a cross-referencing system incorporating the following:

- *sales day book – SDB 55*
  sales returns day book – SRDB 10

- ***sales (debtors) ledger account numbers***
  Dines Stores – account no 86
  Meadow Golf Club – account no 135
  Raven Retailers Ltd – account no 170
  Teme Sports Ltd – account no 178
  Wyvern Stores – account no 195

- ***general (main) ledger account numbers***
  sales account – account no 4001
  sales returns account – account no 4010
  Value Added Tax account – account no 2200

3.4 Pensax Products Limited manufactures plastic goods which are sold direct to shops. During November 2001 the following credit transactions took place:

2001	
3 Nov	Sold goods to Dines Stores £265 + VAT, invoice no 3592
5 Nov	Sold goods to Raven Retailers Limited, £335 + VAT, invoice no 3593
6 Nov	Sold goods to Meadow Golf Club £175 + VAT, invoice no 3594
10 Nov	Sold goods to Wyvern Stores £455 + VAT, invoice no 3595
11 Nov	Sold goods to Dines Stores £290 + VAT, invoice no 3596
13 Nov	Sold goods to Teme Sports Limited £315 + VAT, invoice no 3597
17 Nov	Sold goods to Raven Retailers Limited £1,120 + VAT, invoice no 3598
19 Nov	Sold goods to Teme Sports Limited £825 + VAT, invoice no 3599
21 Nov	Sold goods to Dines Stores £354 + VAT, invoice no 3600
24 Nov	Sold goods to Meadow Golf Club £248 + VAT, invoice no 3601
27 Nov	Sold goods to Wyvern Stores £523 + VAT, invoice no 3602
28 Nov	Sold goods to Raven Retailers Limited £187 + VAT, invoice no 3603

You are to:

(a) enter the above transactions in Pensax Products' sales day book for November 2001

(b) record the accounting entries in Pensax Products' sales ledger and general ledger

3.5 The following details are the sales returns for Pensax Products for November 2001. They are to be

(a) entered in the sales returns day book for November 2001

(b) recorded in the sales ledger and general ledger (use the ledgers already prepared in the answer to Activity 3.4)

2001	
10 Nov	Dines Stores returns goods £55 + VAT, credit note no CN 831 is issued
14 Nov	Wyvern Stores returns goods £60 + VAT, credit note no CN 832 is issued
19 Nov	Meadow Golf Club returns goods £46 + VAT, credit note no CN 833 is issued
24 Nov	Teme Sports Limited returns goods £127 + VAT, credit note no CN 834 is issued
28 Nov	Dines Stores returns goods £87 + VAT, credit note no CN 835 is issued

3.6 John Green runs a wholesale nursery where he grows plants, shrubs and trees. These are sold on credit to garden centres, shops, and local authorities. His book-keeper records sales in an analysed sales day book including columns for VAT, net, plants, shrubs, trees. During April 2001 the following credit transactions took place:

2001	
2 Apr	Sold trees to Wyvern Council £550 + VAT, invoice no 2741
4 Apr	Sold plants to Mereford Garden Centre £345 + VAT, invoice no 2742
7 Apr	Sold trees £155 and shrubs £265 (both + VAT) to JJ Gardening Services, invoice no 2743
10 Apr	Sold shrubs to Mereford Garden Centre, £275 + VAT, invoice no 2744
11 Apr	Sold plants to Dines Stores £127 + VAT, invoice no 2745
15 Apr	Sold shrubs £127 and plants £352 (both + VAT) to Wyvern Council, invoice no 2746
17 Apr	Sold plants to Harford Post Office £228 + VAT, invoice no 2247
23 Apr	Sold trees to Mereford Garden Centre £175 + VAT, invoice no 2748
25 Apr	Sold plants to Bourne Supplies £155 + VAT, invoice no 2749
29 Apr	Sold trees £265 and plants £451 (both + VAT) to Mereford Garden Centre, invoice no 2750

You are to:

(a) enter the above transactions into page 76 of the *analysed* sales day book of John Green

(b) total the day book at 30 April 2001

Notes:

- folio entries are *not* required
- entries in the sales (debtors) ledger and general (main) ledger are *not* required.

4 RECEIVING AND RECORDING PAYMENTS

4.1 You are operating a cash till at the firm where you work. Today the cash float at the start of the day is £22.30, made up as follows:

2 x £5 notes	=	£10.00
6 x £1 coins	=	£6.00
6 x 50p coins	=	£3.00
8 x 20p coins	=	£1.60
10 x 10p coins	=	£1.00
8 x 5p coins	=	£0.40
12 x 2p coins	=	£0.24
6 x 1p coins	=	£0.06
		£22.30

The following are the sales which pass through the till today:

		Amount of sales £	*Notes and/or coin tendered*
Customer	1	7.50	£10 note
	2	3.38	£5 note
	3	2.29	two £1 coins and a 50p coin
	4	18.90	£20 note
	5	6.04	£10 note, £1 coin, two 2p coins
	6	26.36	three £10 notes
	7	4.30	four £1 coins and a 50p coin

You are to:

(a) state the amount of change to be given to each customer

(b) state the notes and/or coin that will be given in change, using the minimum number possible

(c) calculate the denominations of notes and coin that will remain in the till at the end of the day

(d) retain a cash float which does not exceed £30.00 (show the denominations of notes and coin); the remainder of the cash is to be banked (show denominations)

(e) prepare a summary of the day's transactions in the following form:

		£
	cash float at start	22.30
plus	sales made during the day	
equals	amount of cash held at end of day	
less	cash float retained for next day	
	amount banked	

4.2 You work as an accounts assistant in the Accounts Department of Mercia Pumps Ltd, Unit 13, Severn Trading Estate, Mereford MR3 4GF. Today is 3 April 2001. In the morning's post are a number of cheques enclosed with remittance advices. These cheques are illustrated below.

Examine the cheques carefully, and identify any problems, and state what action (if any) you will take, and why. Draft letters where appropriate for your Manager's (Mrs D Strong) signature.

You note from your records that the addresses are as follows:

(a) The Accounts Department, A & S Systems, 5 High Street, Mereford MR1 2JF

(b) Mrs P Thorne, Hillside Cottage, Mintfield, MR4 9HG

(c) The Accounts Department, C Darwin Ltd, 89 Baker Street, Mereford MR2 6RG

(d) Mr I M King, 56 Beaconsfield Drive, Pershore MR7 5GF

(a)

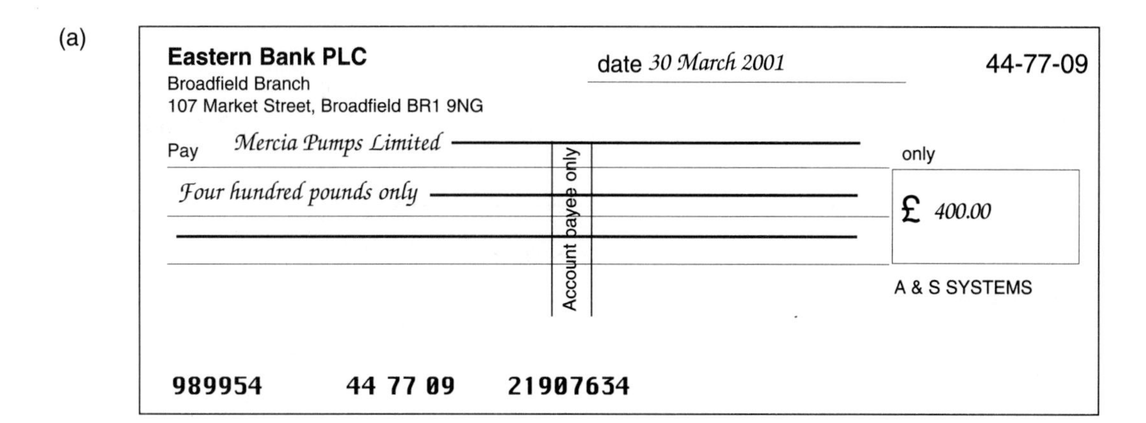
Eastern Bank PLC
Broadfield Branch
107 Market Street, Broadfield BR1 9NG

date *30 March 2001*

44-77-09

Pay *Mercia Pumps Limited*

Account payee only

only

Four hundred pounds only

£ *400.00*

A & S SYSTEMS

989954 44 77 09 21907634

(b)

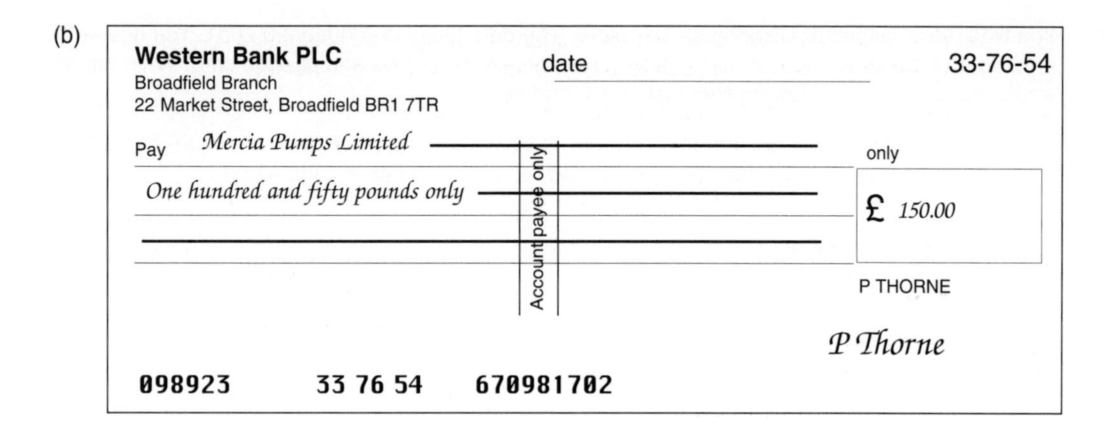

Western Bank PLC
Broadfield Branch
22 Market Street, Broadfield BR1 7TR

date

33-76-54

Pay *Mercia Pumps Limited*

One hundred and fifty pounds only

Account payee only

only

£ *150.00*

P THORNE

P Thorne

098923 33 76 54 670981702

(c)

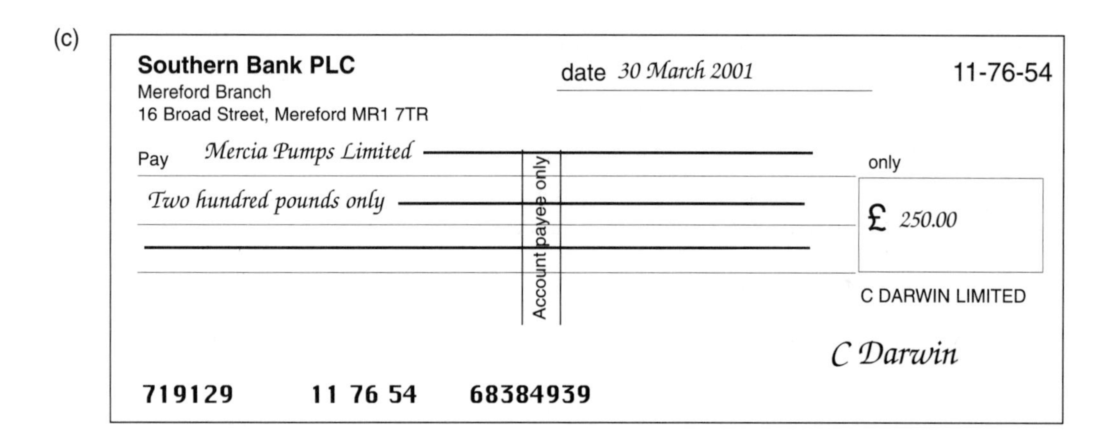

Southern Bank PLC
Mereford Branch
16 Broad Street, Mereford MR1 7TR

date *30 March 2001*

11-76-54

Pay *Mercia Pumps Limited*

Two hundred pounds only

Account payee only

only

£ *250.00*

C DARWIN LIMITED

C Darwin

719129 11 76 54 68384939

(d) Mr King has made the cheque payable to your Sales Director, John Hopkins, who says he is happy to endorse the cheque over to the company.

Northern Bank PLC
Mereford Branch
28 High Street, Mereford MR1 8FD

date *30 March 2001*

22-01-59

Pay *John Hopkins*

Sixty pounds only

Account payee only

only

£ *60.00*

I KING

I M King

123456 22 01 59 37537147

4.3 You work as a cashier at Cripplegate DIY store. The date today is January 20 2001. You deal with a number of customers who wish to make payment using cheques and cheque card. What action would you take in the following circumstances, and why?

(a) Card limit £100, expiry June 2001, code 11-76-54. The name on the card is J E Drew. The lady explains that she has just got married, and Drew is her maiden name.

Southern Bank PLC
Mereford Branch
16 Broad Street, Mereford MR1 7TR

date *20 January 2001* 11-76-54

Pay *Cripplegate DIY* only

Ninety pounds only £ *90.00*

Account payee only

J E DREW

J E Jones

979782 11 76 54 27289931

(b) Card limit £100, expiry May 2001, code 22-01-59. Mr King wants to buy some garden furniture costing £150.95. He has made out the following cheques in advance.

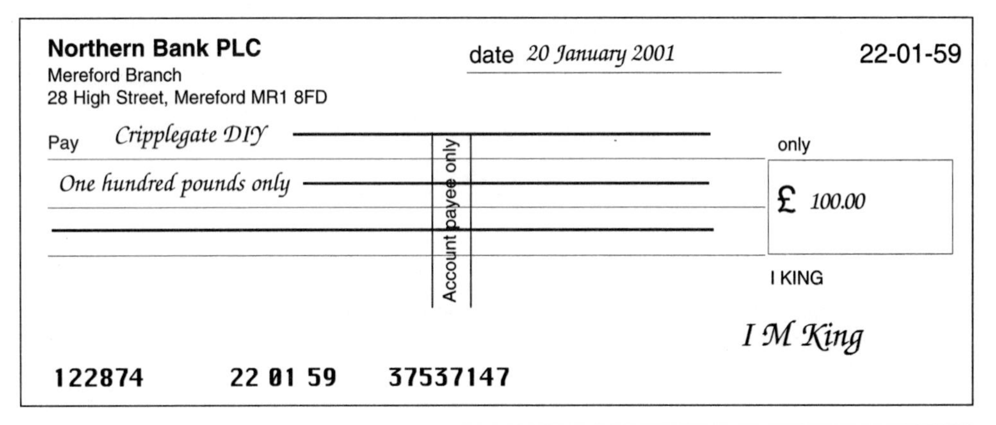

Northern Bank PLC
Mereford Branch
28 High Street, Mereford MR1 8FD

date *20 January 2001* 22-01-59

Pay *Cripplegate DIY* only

One hundred pounds only £ *100.00*

Account payee only

I KING

I M King

122874 22 01 59 37537147

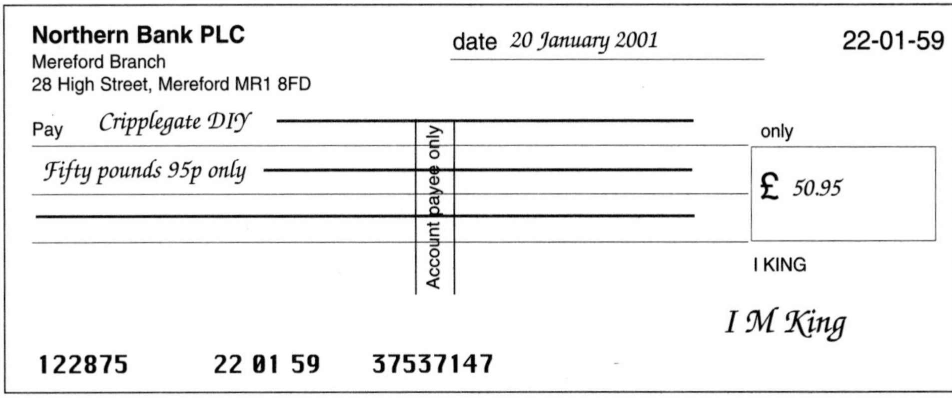

Northern Bank PLC
Mereford Branch
28 High Street, Mereford MR1 8FD

date *20 January 2001* 22-01-59

Pay *Cripplegate DIY* only

Fifty pounds 95p only £ *50.95*

Account payee only

I KING

I M King

122875 22 01 59 37537147

(c) Card limit £200, expiry April 2001, code 33-76-54. The cheque card is handed to you in a plastic wallet and the signature on the card does not quite tally with the signature on the cheque. The customer says that he has sprained his wrist and this has affected his writing.

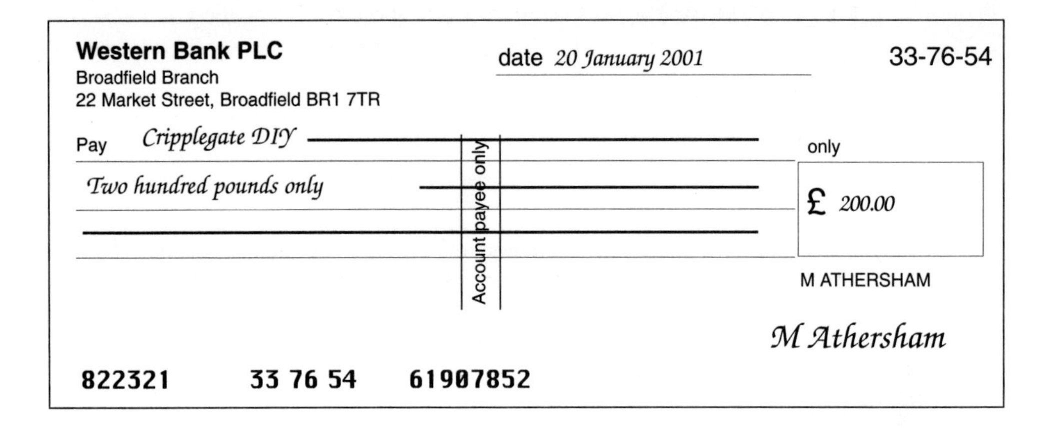
Western Bank PLC
Broadfield Branch
22 Market Street, Broadfield BR1 7TR
date *20 January 2001* 33-76-54
Pay *Cripplegate DIY* only
Two hundred pounds only
Account payee only
£ *200.00*
M ATHERSHAM
M Athersham
822321 33 76 54 61907852

(d) Card limit £200, expiry August 2001, code 88-76-54. Mrs Blackstone is in a great hurry and asks you to be as quick as you can. She seems to be rather agitated. The signature on the cheque matches the signature on the card and everything else seems to be in order.

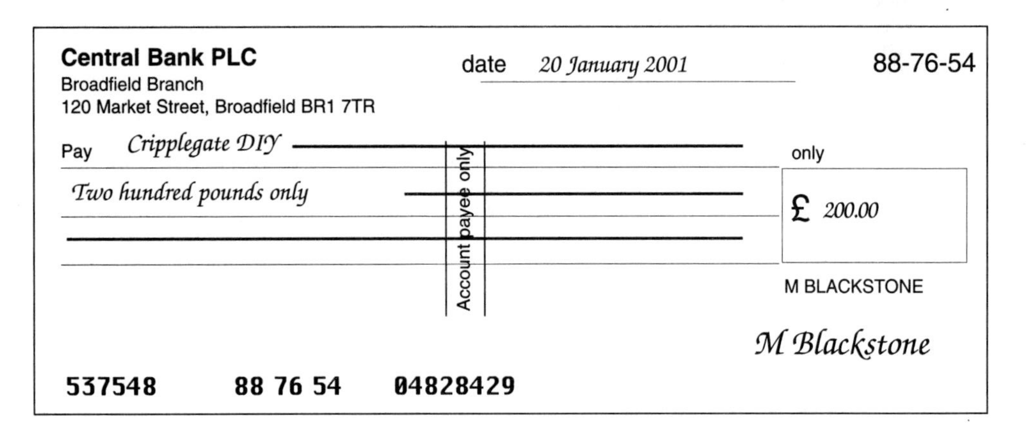
Central Bank PLC
Broadfield Branch
120 Market Street, Broadfield BR1 7TR
date *20 January 2001* 88-76-54
Pay *Cripplegate DIY* only
Two hundred pounds only
Account payee only
£ *200.00*
M BLACKSTONE
M Blackstone
537548 88 76 54 04828429

5 PAYING INTO THE BANK

5.1 You are working in the accounts department of Martley Fruits Limited, Maytree Farm, Martley MR7 2LX. Part of your job is to deal with the cheques received in the post, and to prepare those cheques for banking. During the course of a working day you deal with a number of cheques, some of which may cause problems. Your supervisor, Mark Tucker, asks you to identify the problems, and state in each case how you would deal with them. Write down your answers using the schedule on the next page.

	customer	*amount*	*comments*
(a)	Henry Young & Co	£1,245	you need to find out whether this cheque is to be paid before you can despatch the goods – rapid clearance is required
(b)	J Maxwell Ltd	£124.90	you receive this cheque from the bank; it is marked 'Refer to Drawer'
(c)	Ivor Longway	£342.90	the date on the cheque is three months old
(d)	Ned Morgan	£837.89	the date on the cheque is ten months old
(e)	Lisa Jones	£90.00	you receive this cheque from the bank; the cheque is marked 'Post dated'; on inspecting the cheque you see that the cheque is dated three months in the future
(f)	N Patel	£78.00	you receive this cheque from the bank; it is marked 'Payment Countermanded by order of Drawer'
(g)	N Trebbiano	£78.98	there is no crossing on the cheque

When you have checked your answer schedule with your tutor you are to draft appropriate letters for your supervisor's signature to the following customers (use today's date):

J Maxwell Ltd, 67 The Circus, Bradstreet, BD5 8GY

Ned Morgan, 72 Malvern Crescent, Milton Park, MR6 2CS

Lisa Jones, c/o The Kings Arms, Leatherton, MR6 9SD

customer	problem	solution
Henry Young & Co		
J Maxwell Ltd		
Ivor Longway		
Ned Morgan		
Lisa Jones		
N Patel		
N Trebbiano		

5.2 You are working in the Accounts Department of Wyvern (Office Products) Limited and have been handed the latest bank statement by your supervisor, Alfred Hunter. He asks you to sort out two queries:

- The credit paid in on 1 April appears as £485.02; your paying slip shows the total as £485.04.
- What is the unpaid item on 7 April? Nothing has yet been received from the bank.

The relevant documentation appears on this and the next page.

NATIONAL BANK PLC **Statement of Account**

Branch: Mereford

Account: Wyvern (Office Products) Ltd

Account no 01099124 Sheet no 105 Statement date 10 Apr 2001

Date	Details	Withdrawals	Deposits	Balance
2001		£	£	£
1 Apr	Balance brought forward			1,300.00 Cr
1 Apr	Credit		2,000.00	3,300.00 Cr
1 Apr	BACS Prime Hotels Ltd		2,000.00	5,300.00 Cr
1 Apr	Credit		485.02	5,785.02 Cr
3 Apr	Bank charges	70.00		5,715.02 Cr
7 Apr	Unpaid cheque	2,000.00		3,715.02 Cr
10 Apr	Cheque 123745	1,860.00		1,855.02 Cr

SO Standing Order **DD** Direct Debit **TR** Transfer **BGC** Bank giro credit **BACS** Automated transfer

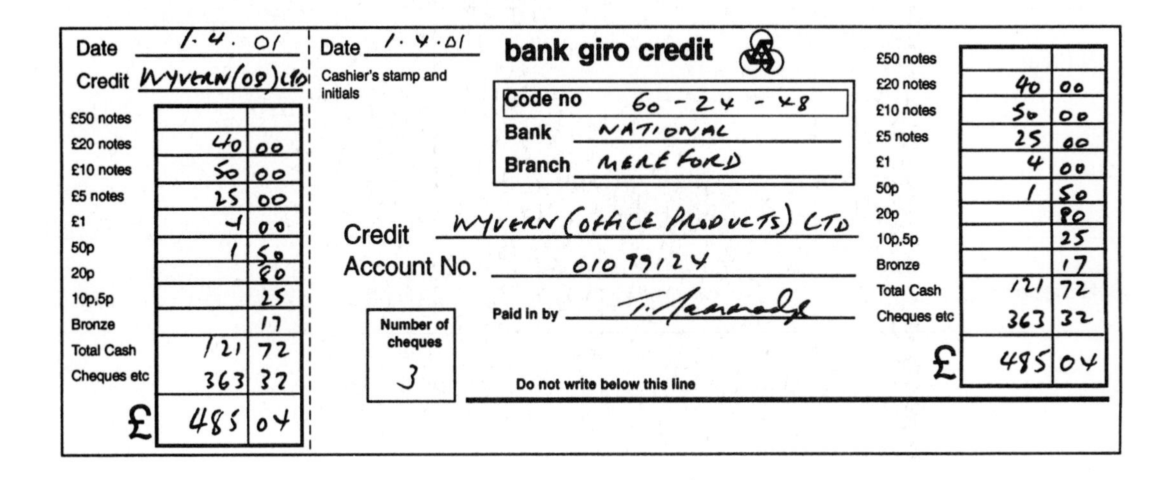

Date 1.4.01

Credit WYVERN (OP) LTD

£50 notes		
£20 notes	40	00
£10 notes	50	00
£5 notes	25	00
£1	4	00
50p	1	50
20p		80
10p,5p		25
Bronze		17
Total Cash	121	72
Cheques etc	363	32
£	485	04

Date 1.4.01

Cashier's stamp and initials

bank giro credit

Code no 60 - 24 - 48

Bank NATIONAL

Branch MEREFORD

Credit WYVERN (OFFICE PRODUCTS) LTD

Account No. 01099124

Number of cheques 3

Paid in by T. [signature]

Do not write below this line

£50 notes		
£20 notes	40	00
£10 notes	50	00
£5 notes	25	00
£1	4	00
50p	1	50
20p		80
10p,5p		25
Bronze		17
Total Cash	121	72
Cheques etc	363	32
£	485	04

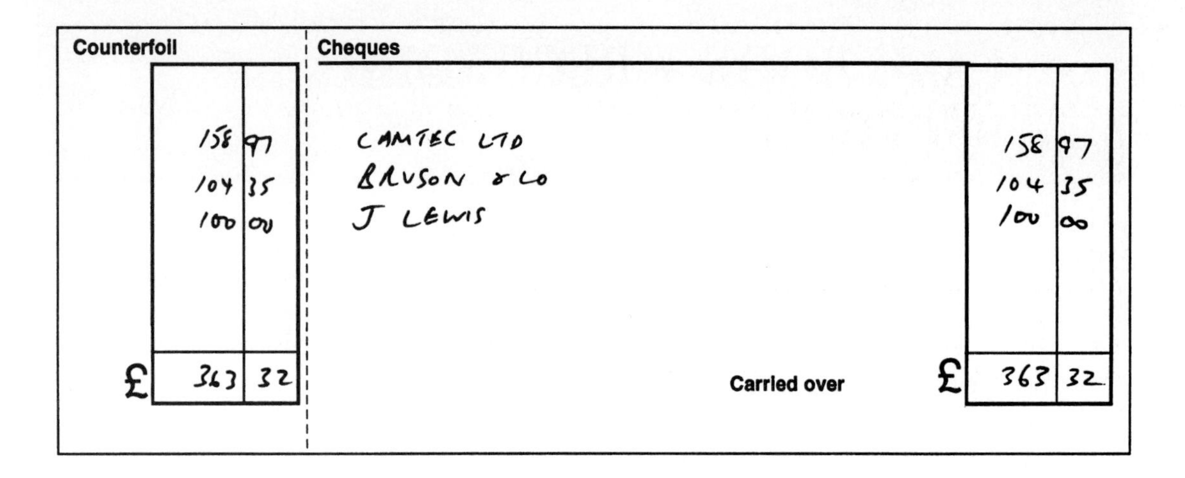

Counterfoil			Cheques		
	158	97	CAMTEC LTD	158	97
	104	35	BRUSON & CO	104	35
	100	00	J LEWIS	100	00
£	363	32	Carried over £	363	32

REMITTANCE ADVICE
BRUSON & CO
25 Melody Chambers, Gloucester GL1 2RF
Tel 01452 37232182 Fax 01452 37234496

Wyvern (Office Products) Ltd
12 Lower Hyde Street
Mereford MR1 2JF

Cheque No 774474
Date 18 February 2001
Account 2947

date	our ref.	your ref.	amount	discount	payment
16.3.01	8274	35357	104.33	00.00	104.33

cheque value £ 104.33

You are to

(a) Write a memorandum to your supervisor explaining what has happened in relation to the paying-in slip and the bank statement.

(b) Write down in numbered points what actions you think should be taken as a result of the mistake on the credit.

(c) Write down in numbered points what actions you think should be taken as a result of the unpaid cheque.

6 CASH BOOK – RECORDING RECEIPTS

6.1 The discount allowed column of the cash book is totalled at regular intervals and transferred to:

(a) the credit side of discount allowed account

(b) the debit side of discount allowed account

(c) the debit side of sales account

(d) the credit side of sales account

Answer (a) or (b) or (c) or (d)

6.2 The VAT column on the receipts side of the cash book is totalled at regular intervals and transferred to:

(a) the debit side of sales returns account

(b) the debit side of VAT account

(c) the credit side of sales account

(d) the credit side of VAT account

Answer (a) or (b) or (c) or (d)

6.3 The following are the receipts transactions of Marcle Enterprises for October 2001:

1 Oct	Balances from previous month: cash £280, bank £2,240
4 Oct	Received a cheque from a debtor, M Perry Limited, £475
5 Oct	Sales for cash, £240 + VAT
9 Oct	Transferred £500 to the bank from cash
11 Oct	Received a bank giro credit for £1,295 from T Francis Limited in full settlement of their account of £1,305
15 Oct	Sales for cash, £320 + VAT
17 Oct	Received a cheque for £640 from H Watson, in full settlement of her account of £660
18 Oct	Received a loan of £1,000 from the bank (no VAT)
22 Oct	Sales £480 + VAT, received half in cash, and half by cheque
24 Oct	Rent received from tenant, £150 in cash (no VAT)
30 Oct	Received a cheque for £464 from M Perry Limited in full settlement of their account of £480
31 Oct	Received £300 in cash which has been withdrawn from the bank for use in the business

The rate of Value Added Tax is 17.5%
All cheques are banked on the day of receipt
Account numbers are to be used – see below

You are to:

- Enter the above receipts on page 67 of the three column cash book of Marcle Enterprises.
- Sub-total the money columns at 31 October.
- Show the entries to be made in the following accounts:

  sales (debtors) ledger
  T Francis Limited (account no 445)
  M Perry Limited (account no 675)
  H Watson (account no 840)
  general (main) ledger
  discount allowed account (account no 6501)
  bank loan (account no 2210)
  rent received account (account no 4951)
  sales account (account no 4001)
  VAT account (account no 2200)

6.4 The following are the receipts transactions of Kendrick and Company for November 2001:

1 Nov	Balances from previous month: cash £125, bank £1,529
5 Nov	D McNamara, a debtor, settles an invoice for £100, paying £95 in cash and receiving £5 discount for prompt settlement
7 Nov	Cash sales £235 (including Value Added Tax) received by cheque
8 Nov	Transferred £400 to the bank from cash
12 Nov	Rent received from tenant, £200 by cheque (no VAT)
15 Nov	Cash sales of £423 (including Value Added Tax) received by cheque
19 Nov	Received a cheque for £595 from Johnson & Co, a debtor, in full settlement of their account of £610
20 Nov	Cash sales of £94 (including Value Added Tax) received in cash
23 Nov	Received £300 in cash which has been withdrawn from the bank for use in the business
26 Nov	Received a cheque for £475 from Mendez Limited, in full settlement of their account of £500
28 Nov	Additional capital paid in, £2,500 by cheque (no VAT)

The rate of Value Added Tax is 17.5%
All cheques are banked on the day of receipt
Account numbers are to be used – see below

You are to:

- Enter the above receipts on page 24 of the cash book of Kendrick and Company, using columns for date, details, discount allowed, VAT, cash and bank.
- Sub-total the money columns at 30 November.
- Show the entries to be made in the following accounts:

sales (debtors) ledger

Johnson & Co (account no 355)

D McNamara (account no 460)

Mendez Limited (account no 505)

general (main) ledger

capital account (account no 3005)

discount allowed account (account no 6501)

rent received account (account no 4951)

sales account (account no 4001)

VAT account (account no 2200)

6.5 Martin Peters runs a building supplies company. He buys in bulk from manufacturers and sells in smaller quantities to trade customers on credit and to the public on cash terms. His business is registered for VAT.

He uses a cash book which analyses receipts between:

- discount allowed
- VAT
- sales
- sales (debtors) ledger
- sundry

The following transactions take place during the week commencing 19 November 2001:

19 Nov	Balances from previous week: cash £384.21, bank £2,576.80
19 Nov	Sales £354.25 (including VAT), cheques received
20 Nov	Received a cheque for £678.11 from Barbourne Builders in full settlement of their account of £695.50
20 Nov	Sales £254.88 (including VAT), cash received
21 Nov	Rent received from tenant of part of the premises, £285.75 by cheque (no VAT)

21 Nov	Sales £476.29 (including VAT), cheques received
21 Nov	Martin Peters pays in additional capital of £2,500.00 by cheque (no VAT)
22 Nov	Sales £351.48 (including VAT), cash received
22 Nov	Received £200.00 in cash which has been withdrawn from the bank for use in the business
23 Nov	A debtor, J Johnson, settles an invoice for £398.01, paying £389.51 by cheque, £8.50 discount being allowed for prompt settlement
23 Nov	Sales £487.29 (including VAT), cheques received
23 Nov	A debtor, Wyvern Council settles an invoice for £269.24 by cheque

The rate of Value Added Tax is 17.5%

All cheques are banked on the day of receipt

Account numbers are to be used – see below

You are to:

- Enter the above receipts on page 45 of the analysed cash book of Martin Peters (VAT amounts should be rounded down to the nearest penny).
- Sub-total the money columns at 23 November.
- Show the entries to be made in the following accounts:

sales (debtors) ledger

Barbourne Builders (account no 115)

J Johnson (account no 497)

Wyvern Council (account no 924)

general (main) ledger

capital account (account no 3005)

discount allowed account (account no 6501)

rent received account (account no 4951)

sales account (account no 4001)

VAT account (account no 2200)

7 DOCUMENTS - BUYING ON CREDIT

7.1 You have just started work as an accounts assistant in the purchasing department of Litho Printers. Your supervisor has asked you to buy 150 reams (a ream is 500 sheets) of standard quality white A4 copy paper. He said "shop around if you can – prices can vary a lot."

You have telephoned four different stationery suppliers for their stationery catalogues and have made enquiries about special offers on copy paper. The best deals seem to be from Saxon Supplies. An extract from their catalogue (which they have faxed through) is shown below.

SAXON SUPPLIES

Unit 12 Hereward Industrial Estate, Warborough, WA3 5TG

Tel 01807 282482 Fax 01807 282412 Email JJ@Saxon.u-net-com.uk

BARGAINS OF THE MONTH!

reference	*product*	*unit*	*list price (VAT excl)*	*sale price (VAT excl)*
RCA4	A4 Roxo 80gsm copy paper (white only) standard quality	ream	3.49	2.79
REFA4	A4 Roxo 80gsm copy paper (white – extra fine quality)	ream	4.99	3.49
RLA4	A4 Roxo 80gsm laser paper	ream	5.49	4.99
CCA4	Colour 80gsm copy paper Add code to your order ref: R (red) B (blue) Y (yellow)	ream	5.50	4.50
EWDLP	White self-seal DL envelopes (plain)	1000 box	25.00	10.99
EWDLSS	White self-seal DL envelopes (window)	1000 box	35.00	16.99
N1	'Nifty' air bubble mail envelopes 200mm x 300mm	100 box	22.00	18.00
N2	'Nifty' air bubble mail envelopes 235mm x 370mm	100 box	25.00	21.00
FR15	Fax roll 210mm x 15m	roll	2.85	1.50
FR30	Fax roll 216mm x 30m	roll	5.00	3.50

Your supervisor, who has seen the Saxon Supplies prices, says that she also wants to order 50 fax rolls (30m) and 5 boxes of white self-seal DL window envelopes which are used to send out customer statements.

You are to complete the purchase order shown below for the 150 reams of ordinary white copy paper and the extra items requested by the supervisor. You are authorised to sign the order (use your own name). Saxon Supplies has said over the telephone that you can have an initial 15% discount on all orders. The purchase order number is 2892. The date is 8 December 2001.

PURCHASE ORDER

litho printers

Unit 7 Buttermere Estate
Station Road
Broadfield
BR6 3TR
Tel 01908 456291 Fax 01908 456913

to

purchase order no

date

product code	quantity	description

Authorised signature..date...

3.2 Later in the morning you have to check a delivery note for goods just received against the original purchase order (see page 40). Write a letter to the supplier (see page 41) explaining what is wrong with the delivery. Use your own name and the title 'Accounts Assistant'. The date is 8 December 2001.

PURCHASE ORDER

litho printers

Unit 7 Buttermere Estate
Station Road
Broadfield
BR6 3TR
Tel 01908 456291 Fax 01908 456913

to

Eleco Supplies
79 Broadacre
Boreham
BO7 6TG

purchase order no 3601

date 20 November 2001

product code	quantity	description
23477C	5	Typo office chairs, charcoal

Authorised signature *A Morello* date *20.1101*

DELIVERY NOTE

eleco supplies

79 Broadacre
Boreham
BO7 6TG
Tel 01208 070111 Fax 01208 070149

to

Litho Printers Limited
Unit 7 Buttermere Estate
Station Road
Broadfield
BR6 3TR

Delivery Note No 39823
Purchase Order no 3601
Date 5 December 2001
Delivery Lightning Carriers

product code	quantity	description
22477C	5	Executive chairs, charcoal

Received in good condition

signature *R Smithers* date *8.12.01*

litho printers

Unit 7 Buttermere Estate, Station Road,
Broadfield BR6 3TR
Tel 01908 456291 Fax 01908 456913
E-mail ben@litho.u-net.com

Litho Printers Limited. Registered office: Unit 7 Buttermere Estate, Station Road, Broadfield BR6 3TR
Registered in England No 3539857. VAT Reg GB 32 73687 78

3.3 After lunch on the same day (8 December 2001) you have to check three incoming invoices against the appropriate goods received notes which have been raised (see pages 42 to 44). They should be checked for accuracy and to make sure that they apply to the goods supplied. You are to make a list of any errors or discrepancies and pass it to your supervisor on the schedule on page 45. Each of the suppliers normally gives 20% trade discount, but no cash discount.

INVOICE

JUMBO STATIONERY

91 HIGH STREET, BROADFIELD, BR7 4ER
Tel 01908 129426 Fax 01908 129919

invoice to

Litho Printers Limited
Unit 7 Buttermere Estate
Station Road
Broadfield BR6 3TR

invoice no 234672
account 2984
your reference 3627
date/tax point 1 December 2001

product code	description	quantity	price	unit	total	discount %	net
JB234	Jetstream Biros, finepoint, black	20	2.25	box	45.00	10	40.50

terms
Net monthly
Carriage paid
E & OE

goods total	40.50
VAT	7.08
TOTAL	47.58

JAVELIN OFFICE MACHINES

invoice

Unit 19 Elgar Estate, Broadfield, BR7 4ER
Tel 01908 765101 Fax 01908 765304

invoice to

Litho Printers Limited
Unit 7 Buttermere Estate
Station Road
Broadfield BR6 3TR

invoice no 10483
account 935
order reference 3629
date/tax point 2 December 2001

product code	description	quantity	price	unit	total	discount %	net
M17C	Multipoint 17" colour monitor	1	499.00	item	499.00	20	399.20

terms
Net monthly
Carriage paid
E & OE

goods total	399.20
VAT	69.86
TOTAL	469.06

EDWARD HUGHES LIMITED **invoice**

Unit 3 Bronglais Estate, Pwllmadoc, LL1 4ER
Tel 01708 323242 Fax 01708 323242 VAT Reg GB 5019 46 2

invoice to

Litho Printers Limited
Unit 7 Buttermere Estate
Station Road
Broadfield BR6 3TR

invoice no 12931
account 9742
your reference 3628
date/tax point 2 December 2001

product code	description	quantity	price	unit	total	discount %	net
3883	Automatic offset crimper	1	8295.00	unit	8295.00	20	6636.00

terms
Net monthly
Carriage paid
E & OE

goods total	6636.00
VAT	1116.30
TOTAL	7752.30

litho printers **GOODS RECEIVED NOTE**

GRN no. 301
supplier Jumbo Stationery
date 3 December 2001

order ref.	quantity	description
3627	15 boxes	Jetstream biros (fine point, black)

received by *R Nixon* ..... checked by *I Singh* .....

condition of goods good 15 boxes
damages
shortages 5 boxes

litho printers — **GOODS RECEIVED NOTE**

GRN no. 303
supplier Javelin Office Machines
date 4 December 2001

order ref.	quantity	description
3629	1	Multipoint 17 inch colour monitor

received by *J Kennedy* checked by *I Singh*

condition of goods good √
damages
shortages

litho printers — **GOODS RECEIVED NOTE**

GRN no. 302
supplier Edward Hughes Ltd
date 4 December 2001

order ref.	quantity	description
3628	1	Automatic offset crimper

received by *J Kennedy* checked by *M Jones*

condition of goods good √
damages
shortages

date	Order no.	Action to be taken

3.4 Today it is 12 December 2001 and the stationery order from Saxon Supplies (see Task 3.1) has arrived. The goods received note shows that the correct quantity of goods has been received and that there are no wrong goods or damaged items.

You have now been passed the invoice for checking against the original order (produced in Task 3.1). If there are any problems with the invoice, write them down on the memorandum on the next page. Address the memo to your supervisor, James Ridelle. Use your own name. Your title is Accounts Assistant.

INVOICE

SAXON SUPPLIES

Unit 12 Hereward Industrial Estate, Warborough, WA3 5TG

Tel 01807 282482 Fax 01807 282412 Email JJ@Saxon.u-net-com.uk

invoice to

Litho Printers Limited
Unit 7 Buttermere Estate
Station Road
Broadfield BR6 3TR

invoice no	89422
account	230
your reference	2892
date/tax point	10 December 2001

product code	description	quantity	price	unit	total	discount %	net
RCA4	A4 Roxo 80gsm copy paper	150	3.49	ream	523.50	15	444.98
FR30	Fax roll 216mm x 30mm	50	3.50	unit	175.00	15	148.75
EWDLSS	White self-seal window DL envelopes	5	16.99	box	84.95	15	72.21

goods total	665.94
VAT	116.53
TOTAL	782.47

terms
Net monthly
Carriage paid
E & OE

MEMORANDUM

date
to
from
subject

8 ACCOUNTING FOR CREDIT PURCHASES AND PURCHASES RETURNS

8.1 Which one shows the correct accounting entries to record the purchase of goods for resale on credit?

	Debit	Credit
(a)	purchases returns account	supplier's account
(b)	purchases account	supplier's account
(c)	supplier's account	purchases returns account
(d)	supplier's account	purchases account

Answer (a) or (b) or (c) or (d)

In the activities which follow, the rate of Value Added Tax is to be calculated at the current rate (17.5% at the time of writing). When calculating VAT amounts, you should ignore fractions of a penny, ie round down to a whole penny.

For activities 8.2 and 8.3 use a cross-referencing system incorporating the following:

purchases day book – *PDB 36*
purchases returns day book – *PRDB 11*

purchases (creditors) ledger account numbers

S Burston – *account no 530*
Iley Wholesalers – *account no 605*
Malvern Manufacturing – *account no 625*
SG Enterprises – *account no 720*

general (main) ledger accounts

purchases account – *account no 5001*
purchases returns account – *account no 5010*
Value Added Tax account – *account no 2200*

8.2 During July 2001, Tyax Trading Company had the following transactions:

2001

3 Jul	Bought goods from Malvern Manufacturing £170 +VAT, invoice no I7321
9 Jul	Bought goods from S Burston £265 +VAT, invoice SB745
12 Jul	Bought goods from Iley Wholesalers £450 +VAT, invoice no I4721
18 Jul	Bought goods from SG Enterprises £825 +VAT, invoice no 3947
23 Jul	Bought goods from S Burston £427 +VAT, invoice no SB773
30 Jul	Bought goods from Malvern Manufacturing £364 +VAT, invoice no I7408

You are to:

(a) enter the above transactions in Tyax Trading Company's purchases day book for July 2001

(b) record the accounting entries in Tyax Trading Company's purchases ledger and general ledger

8.3 The following are the purchases returns of Tyax Trading Company for July 2001. They are to be:

(a) entered in the purchases returns day book for July 2001

(b) recorded in the purchases ledger and general ledger (use the ledgers already prepared in the answer to Activity 8.2).

2001

11 Jul	Returned goods to Malvern Manufacturing £70 +VAT, credit note no CN345 received
17 Jul	Returned goods to Iley Wholesalers for £85 +VAT, credit note no CN241 received
24 Jul	Returned goods to SG Enterprises for £25 +VAT, credit note no 85 received
31 Jul	Returned goods to S Burston for £55 +VAT, credit note no 295 received

8.4 The Oasis Trading Company records its credit purchases in an analysed day book with the following headings: VAT, net, goods for resale, printing, telephone. The transactions for March 2001 are as follows:

2001

3 Mar	Bought goods for resale from Severn Valley Traders £255.50 + VAT, invoice no X1247
4 Mar	Bought goods for resale from Mercian Suppliers £356.25 + VAT, invoice no 7977
6 Mar	Received invoice no Z495 for £136.95 + VAT from Print Services Ltd for printing

10 Mar	Bought goods for resale from D James Ltd £368.21 + VAT, invoice no 2461
14 Mar	Received invoice no 769431 for £218.25 + VAT from United Telecom for telephone costs
17 Mar	Bought goods for resale from Wyvern Traders £45.40 + VAT, invoice no A419
19 Mar	Bought goods for resale from A-Z Traders £496.84 + VAT, invoice no AZ 7231
21 Mar	Received invoice no 561742 for £154.65 + VAT from Saturn Communications for telephone costs
24 Mar	Bought goods for resale from A J Knowles £151.20 + VAT, invoice no 2761
25 Mar	Bought goods for resale from Severn Valley Traders £357.24 + VAT, invoice no X1299
28 Mar	Received invoice no 597234 for £121.47 + VAT from Total Communications plc for telephone costs
31 Mar	Received invoice no Z610 for £117.25 from Print Services Ltd for printing

You are to:

- enter the above transactions into an analysed purchases day book
- total the day book at 31 March

Note: Entries in the purchases ledger and general ledger are not required.

9 MAKING PAYMENTS

9.1 You work as an assistant in the accounts department of A & S Systems Limited, computer consultants. Your job is to pay purchase invoices. Your file contains 12 invoices which have all been approved for payment.

The company writes out cheques in settlement of suppliers' invoices every week. It is company policy to pay strictly according to the terms of the invoice and to take advantage of cash discounts whenever possible. Today is 27 March 2001.

You have been on holiday for a fortnight and someone else has done your job the last two weeks. Your supervisor suggests you check carefully to make sure your file is brought up to date and all outstanding invoices are settled, as he suspects some may have been overlooked.

You are to select the invoices due for payment and calculate the amount due on those invoices, taking into account any cash discount. A summary of the invoices is shown below.

invoice date	*supplier*	*terms*	*net*	*VAT*	*invoice total*
			£	£	£
11.02.01	James Smith Ltd	30 days	456.89	79.95	536.84
13.02.01	R Singh	30 days*	1,200.00	204.75	1,404.75
24.02.01	John Hopkins	30 days	230.75	40.38	271.13
24.02.01	Mereford Supplies	60 days	235.00	41.12	276.12
2.03.01	E Ragle Ltd	30 days	345.89	60.53	406.42
23.03.01	Meteor Ltd	30 days*	2,400.00	409.50	2,809.50
16.02.01	Helen Jarvis	30 days	109.00	19.07	128.07
17.02.01	Martley Electronics	60 days	245.00	42.87	287.87
24.03.01	Jones & Co	30 days*	950.00	162.09	1,112.09
20.02.01	J Marvell	30 days	80.95	14.16	95.11
19.02.01	K Nott	60 days	457.50	80.06	537.56
20.03.01	V Williams	30 days	1,250.00	218.75	1,468.75

* These invoices are marked '2.5% cash discount for settlement within 7 days'.

9.2 Complete the cheques shown on this and the next page in settlement of the invoices you have decided to pay. The date today is 27 March 2001. You will not sign the cheques; this will be done by two authorised signatories.

Eastern Bank PLC
Broadfield Branch
107 Market Street, Broadfield BR1 9NG

date ____________ 44-77-09

Pay ____________ Account payee only ____________ only

£

A & S SYSTEMS

989954 44 77 09 21907634

Eastern Bank PLC
Broadfield Branch
107 Market Street, Broadfield BR1 9NG

date ____________ 44-77-09

Pay ____________ Account payee only ____________ only

£

A & S SYSTEMS

989955 44 77 09 21907634

Eastern Bank PLC
Broadfield Branch
107 Market Street, Broadfield BR1 9NG

date ____________ 44-77-09

Pay ____________ Account payee only ____________ only

£

A & S SYSTEMS

989956 44 77 09 21907634

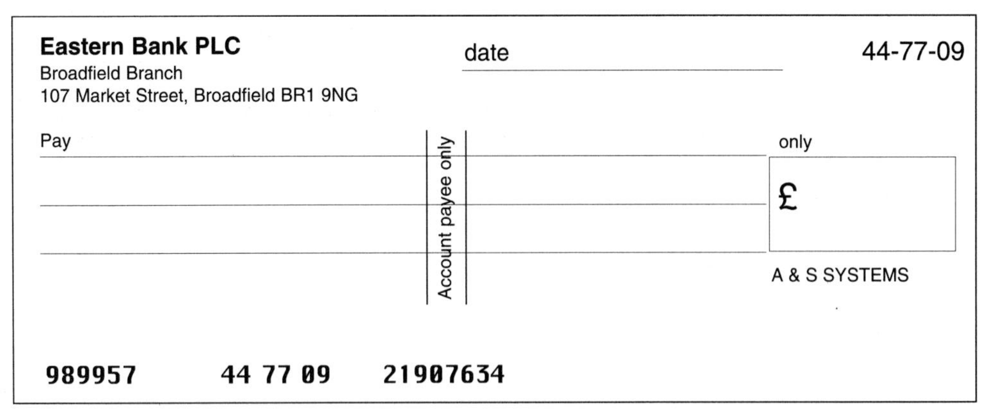

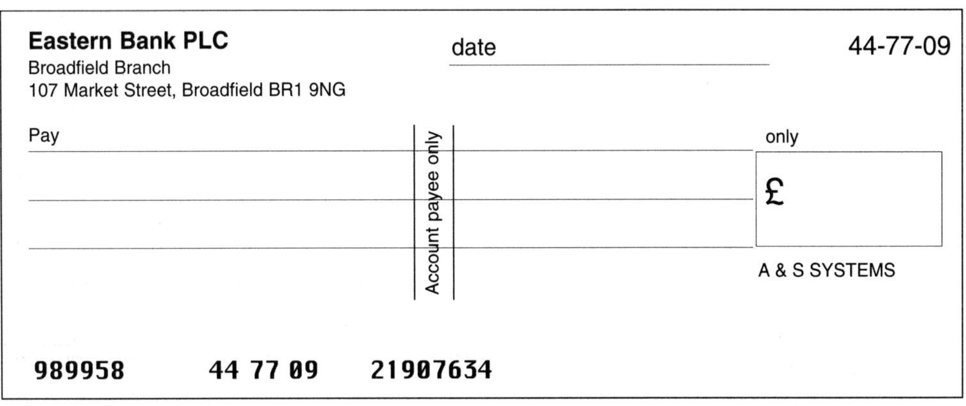

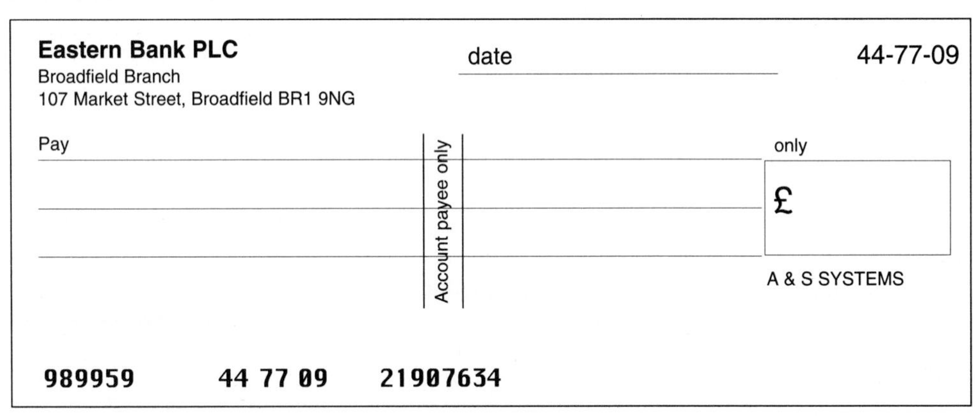

9.3 On 27 March 2001 your supervisor also asks you to arrange three payments: two wages cheques to new employees not yet on the computer payroll and a subscription to a professional organisation. You are to arrange these payments on the documents shown on the next page (you do not need to write out any cheques, or to sign the standing order). The details are as follows:

(a) Wages of £89.00 to R Power at Western Bank, Broadfield, Code 33 76 54, account number 71976234.

(b) Wages of £155.00 to R Patel at Central Bank, Broadfield, Code 88 76 51, account number 04892192.

(c) Monthly subscription of £15.00 (starting 1 April 2001, until further notice) to Association of Software Designers at Eastern Bank, Mereford, 44 77 06, account number 21903461, reference 121092.

Date
Credit

£50 notes		
£20 notes		
£10 notes		
£5 notes		
£1		
50p		
20p		
10p,5p		
Bronze		
Total Cash		
Cheques etc		
£		

Date
Cashier's stamp and initials

bank giro credit

Code no
Bank
Branch

Credit
Account No.

Number of cheques

Paid in by

Do not write below this line

£50 notes		
£20 notes		
£10 notes		
£5 notes		
£1		
50p		
20p		
10p,5p		
Bronze		
Total Cash		
Cheques etc		
£		

Date
Credit

£50 notes		
£20 notes		
£10 notes		
£5 notes		
£1		
50p		
20p		
10p,5p		
Bronze		
Total Cash		
Cheques etc		
£		

Date
Cashier's stamp and initials

bank giro credit

Code no
Bank
Branch

Credit
Account No.

Number of cheques

Paid in by

Do not write below this line

£50 notes		
£20 notes		
£10 notes		
£5 notes		
£1		
50p		
20p		
10p,5p		
Bronze		
Total Cash		
Cheques etc		
£		

Standing Order Mandate

To ______________________ Bank

Address ______________________

Please Pay To

Bank ______________ Branch ______________ Sort code [ ]

Beneficiary ______________________ Account number [ ]

The sum of £ [ ] Amount in words ______________________

Date of first payment ______________ Frequency of payment ______________

Until ______________ Reference ______________

Account to be debited [ ] Account number [ ]

Signature(s) ....

.... date..........................

10 PAYROLL PAYMENTS

10.1 Horne Electronics Limited employs twenty staff on its weekly payroll. They work a basic 35 hour week and are paid time-and-a-half for overtime. The basic pay rates are as follows:

Supervisor £7.50 per hour

Production staff: Grade 1 £6.00 per hour; Grade 2 £5.00 per hour

Clerical staff: Grade 1 £6.00 per hour; Grade 2 £5.50 per hour

During the course of one week the weekly paid staff work the following hours:

SUPERVISORS		PRODUCTION STAFF		CLERICAL STAFF	
J Plant	37 hours	***Grade 1***		***Grade 1***	
R Nott	36 hours	R Singh	35 hours	S Rozier	35 hours
		L Watt	38 hours	H James	36 hours
		J Weston	37 hours	R Pratt	38 hours
		Grade 2		***Grade 2***	
		L Curzon	35 hours	N Tamplin	40 hours
		N Serpel	36 hours	P Sargeant	36 hours
		E Smithson	39 hours	T Rotter	35 hours
		T Rothstein	36 hours	L Purcell	36 hours
		R Peggio	37 hours	R Patel	35 hours
		K West	41 hours	N Moore	37 hours

You are to calculate the gross pay of each weekly paid employee. Use the form on the next page.

employee	basic hours	basic pay £	overtime hours	overtime pay £	total gross pay £
Supervisors					
J Plant					
R Nott					
Production staff					
R Singh					
L Watt					
J Weston					
L Curzon					
N Serpel					
E Smithson					
T Rothstein					
R Peggio					
K West					
Clerical staff					
S Rozier					
H James					
R Pratt					
N Tamplin					
P Sargeant					
T Rotter					
L Purcell					
R Patel					
N Moore					

10.2 Horne Electronics employs ten monthly paid staff who are at executive and managerial levels. They are on the following pay scale:

Scale	*Annual Salary (£)*	*Employees*
1	12,500	T Restdale, Y Crouch, H Perkins, J Hampson
2	15,000	K Pantone, R Pettit
3	17,500	S Matthews, R Forrester
4	20,000	J Wibley
5	25,000	K Horne

It is the first month of the tax year and salaried staff have been given a productivity bonus of 5% of their gross annual salary. They have also been given the overtime shown below.

You are to calculate for each salaried employee:

(a) the basic gross monthly salary of each of the ten salaried staff (round to the nearest penny)

(b) the seasonal bonus

(c) the total gross monthly pay

Use the form set out below.

employee	annual salary £	monthly pay £	overtime £	bonus £	total monthly pay £
T Restdale			45.00		
Y Crouch			65.50		
H Perkins			none		
J Hampson			28.50		
K Pantone			none		
R Pettit			15.50		
S Matthews			16.00		
R Forrester			none		
J Wibley			none		
K Horne			none		

10.3 You are asked to work out the net annual pay of some of the salaried employees of Horne Electronics in Activity 10.2.

They all have a Personal Tax Allowance of £4500 a year.

Tax is payable at 10% on the first £500 of taxable pay and at 22% on the remainder.

They all pay National Insurance Contributions at a rate of 10% per annum on their gross pay apart from the first £350 a month which is free of deductions.

(a) You are to work out their annual net pay on the table set out below

employee	annual gross pay £	annual taxable pay £	tax @10% £	tax @ 22% £	NIC £	annual net pay £
J Hampson	12,500					
K Pantone	15,000					
S Matthews	17,500					
J Wibley	20,000					
K Horne	25,000					

(b) You receive notice from the Inland Revenue that K Horne's tax code has been reduced to 400L, which means that his Personal Allowance is reduced to £4,000 a year. What is his annual net pay after this change?

employee	annual gross pay £	annual taxable pay £	tax @10% £	tax @ 22% £	NIC £	annual net pay £
K Horne	25,000					

10.4 Osborne Electronics has six staff on the weekly payroll, all of whom are paid in cash. You have just drawn up the Week 7 payroll analysis sheet, an extract from which is shown on the next page. You are to complete a cash analysis for the six employees. The highest value notes and coins should be used, but no more than two £50 notes should be included in any pay packet.

OSBORNE ELECTRONICS		payroll analysis sheet									tax week 7	
employee reference	employee name	Earnings				Deductions				Employer's National Insurance Contributions £	Employer's Pension Contributions £	Net Pay £
		Basic £	Overtime £	Bonus £	Total Gross Pay £	Income Tax £	National Insurance £	Pension Contributions £	Total Deductions £			
2345	W Rowberry	205.00	25.00	15.00	245.00	35.00	19.50	10.25	64.75	24.50	10.25	180.25
2346	M Richardson	205.00	10.00	15.00	230.00	32.50	18.00	10.25	60.75	23.05	10.25	169.25
2347	D Stanbury	205.00	35.00	15.00	255.00	37.00	20.50	-	57.50	25.50	-	197.50
2348	D Payne	205.00	25.00	15.00	245.00	35.00	19.50	-	54.50	24.50	-	190.50
2349	K Peters	205.00	10.00	15.00	230.00	32.50	18.00	-	50.50	23.05	-	179.50
2350	O Robinson	205.00	15.00	15.00	235.00	34.00	18.50	10.25	62.75	24.50	10.25	172.25
TOTALS		1230.00	120.00	90.00	1440.00	206.00	114.00	30.75	350.75	145.10	30.75	1089.25

cash analysis sheet tax week..................

OSBORNE ELECTRONICS

name	£50	£20	£10	£5	£2	£1	50p	20p	10p	5p	2p	1p	total
NUMBER													
TOTAL (£.p)													

10.5 Osborne Electronics also has three staff on the weekly payroll who are paid by cheque. You are to make out cheques *ready for signing* for the following employees (use today's date):

F Musgrave	£256.75
H Broadhurst	£189.79
L Wright	£246.43

Western Bank PLC
Worcester Branch
44 High Street, Worcester WR1 9NG

date 75-77-09

Pay

Account payee only

only

£

OSBORNE ELECTRONICS

574583 75 77 09 79108734

Western Bank PLC
Worcester Branch
44 High Street, Worcester WR1 9NG

date 75-77-09

Pay

Account payee only

only

£

OSBORNE ELECTRONICS

574584 75 77 09 79108734

Western Bank PLC
Worcester Branch
44 High Street, Worcester WR1 9NG

date 75-77-09

Pay

Account payee only

only

£

OSBORNE ELECTRONICS

574585 75 77 09 79108734

10.6 Osborne Electronics has just taken on three new staff on the monthly payroll and needs to make payment of their first wages by bank giro credit. The details are:

employee	*bank*	*sort code*	*account no*	*amount (£)*
J Lloyd	HSBC, Stourminster	40 40 40	12826251	189.00
H Thin	Lloyds TSB, Comberton	30 40 50	42447998	175.60
L Bright	Barclays, Bredon	20 87 65	80975132	179.50

Complete the credits and the schedule and cheque (see next page), ready for signature. Date the documents so that the money will reach the accounts on the last working day of the current month.

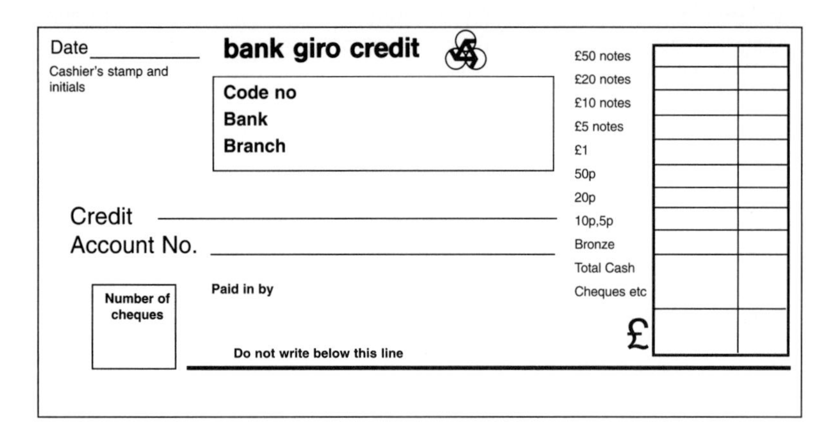

Date__________
Cashier's stamp and initials

bank giro credit

Code no
Bank
Branch

Credit ____________________
Account No. ____________________

Number of cheques

Paid in by

Do not write below this line

£50 notes		
£20 notes		
£10 notes		
£5 notes		
£1		
50p		
20p		
10p,5p		
Bronze		
Total Cash		
Cheques etc		
£		

Date__________
Cashier's stamp and initials

bank giro credit

Code no
Bank
Branch

Credit ____________________
Account No. ____________________

Number of cheques

Paid in by

Do not write below this line

£50 notes		
£20 notes		
£10 notes		
£5 notes		
£1		
50p		
20p		
10p,5p		
Bronze		
Total Cash		
Cheques etc		
£		

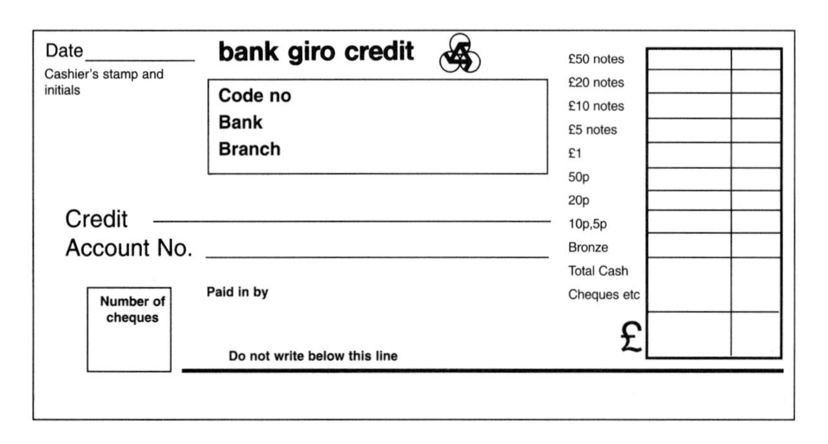

Date__________
Cashier's stamp and initials

bank giro credit

Code no
Bank
Branch

Credit ____________________
Account No. ____________________

Number of cheques

Paid in by

Do not write below this line

£50 notes		
£20 notes		
£10 notes		
£5 notes		
£1		
50p		
20p		
10p,5p		
Bronze		
Total Cash		
Cheques etc		
£		

bank giro credit schedule

To Western Bank PLC

Branch ______________________ Customer account name ______________________

Please distribute the credits listed below. Our cheque for £ ____________ is enclosed.

Signed ____ Date ____________

code	bank and branch	account	amount £
		TOTAL	

Western Bank PLC
Worcester Branch
44 High Street, Worcester WR1 9NG

date ______________________ 75-77-09

Pay ______________________ Account payee only ______________________ only

£

OSBORNE ELECTRONICS

574599 75 77 09 79108734

10.7 The three new staff taken on by Osborne Electronics in Activity 10.6 (page 61) have been placed on a BACS 'auto credit' system. The details of the next month's pay are:

employee	*payee number*	*sort code*	*account no*	*amount (£)*
J Lloyd	456	40 40 40	12826251	786.00
H Thin	457	30 40 50	42447998	899.50
L Bright	458	20 87 65	80975132	885.75

Complete the schedule shown below, ready for signature. The payments should reach the bank accounts on the last working day of the next current month. The company reference is OE3452.

WESTERN BANK PLC
Auto Credit System

Bank branch...

Originator name...Reference................................

Date................................

Branch	*Account no*	*Name*	*Payee no*	*Amount*
		PAYMENT TOTAL		

Please make the above payments to reach the payees on ....(date)

Please debit account no................................with the sum of £...............................

Authorised signature...

10.8 You work in the Wages Office of Weatherbury Publications. It is 8 May 2001, just after the end of tax Month 1, and you have processed the payroll of the staff who are all on a monthly BACS wages payment scheme.

The wages have already been paid and the entries made in the ledger.

You have been allocated the task of making the monthly cheque payment to the Inland Revenue; the payment is due by 19 May.

The payroll summary shows the following figures:

employee	*gross pay* £	*National Insurance* £	*income tax* £
G Oak	1,070.00	192.16	154.84
B Everdene	1,708.23	319.36	301.58
D Venn	1,032.60	184.16	146.10
E Vye	1,433.50	264.16	238.33
S Smith	1,392.50	256.26	228.90
R Priddle	991.40	165.16	136.67
A Clare	1,459.60	269.76	244.31
T Durbeyfield	853.75	115.60	104.93
M South	1,067.00	191.36	154.15
F Day	656.78	76.16	59.62
J Fawley	932.88	164.16	123.10
S Bridehead	1,063.40	190.56	153.25
TOTALS (£)			

You are to

(a) Calculate the totals of the National Insurance and income tax columns on the summary form.

(b) Transfer these totals to the Inland Revenue P30B paying-in slip on the next page. The form should be completed ready for signature and paying in on 14 May.

(c) Complete the cheque on the next page. Make it payable to the Inland Revenue and ready for signature.

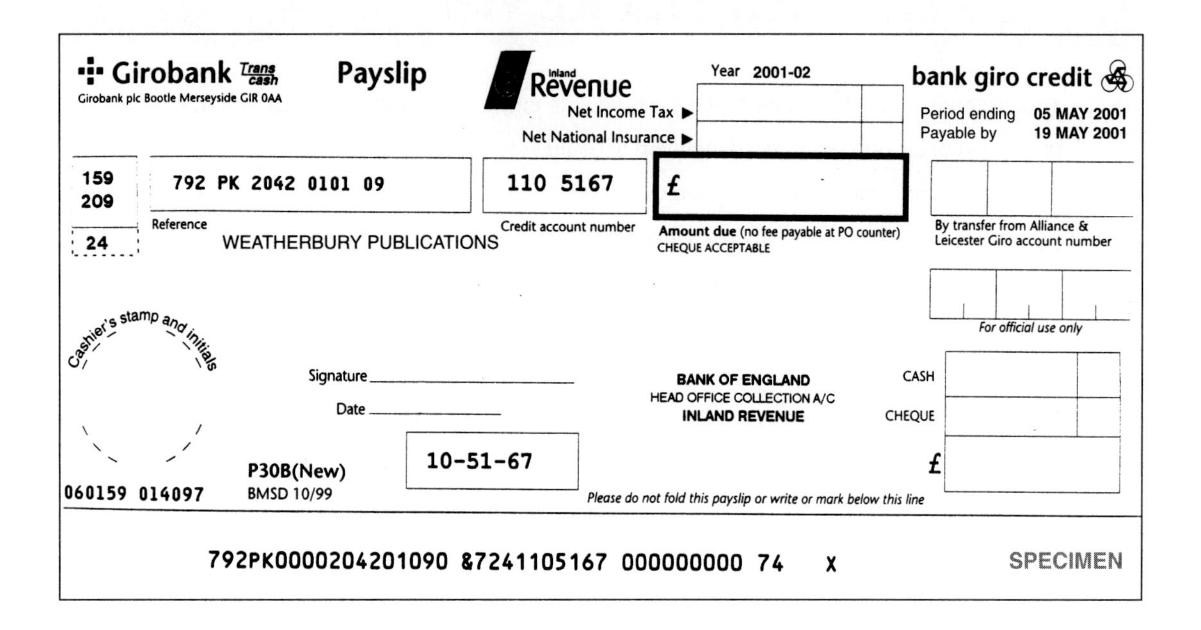

Girobank Transcash
Girobank plc Bootle Merseyside GIR 0AA

Payslip

Inland Revenue

Year 2001-02

Net Income Tax ▶

Net National Insurance ▶

bank giro credit

Period ending 05 MAY 2001
Payable by 19 MAY 2001

159
209
24

792 PK 2042 0101 09
Reference
WEATHERBURY PUBLICATIONS

110 5167
Credit account number

£
Amount due (no fee payable at PO counter)
CHEQUE ACCEPTABLE

By transfer from Alliance & Leicester Giro account number

For official use only

Cashier's stamp and initials

Signature ____________

Date ____________

BANK OF ENGLAND
HEAD OFFICE COLLECTION A/C
INLAND REVENUE

CASH

CHEQUE

£

060159 014097

P30B(New)
BMSD 10/99

10-51-67

Please do not fold this payslip or write or mark below this line

792PK0000204201090 &7241105167 000000000 74 X

SPECIMEN

Western Bank PLC
Casterbridge Branch
12 Cornmarket, Casterbridge NB1 2HG

date 19

75-67-66

Pay

Account payee only

only

£

WEATHERBURY PUBLICATIONS

574599 75 67 66 86721087

11 CASH BOOK – RECORDING PAYMENTS

11.1 The discount received column of the cash book is totalled at regular intervals and transferred to:

(a) the debit side of discount received account

(b) the credit side of discount received account

(c) the credit side of general expenses account

(d) the debit side of general expenses account

Answer (a) or (b) or (c) or (d)

11.2 The VAT column on the payments side of the cash book is totalled at regular intervals and transferred to:

(a) the credit side of VAT account

(b) the credit side of sales account

(c) the debit side of VAT account

(d) the debit side of general expenses account

Answer (a) or (b) or (c) or (d)

11.3 You work as the cashier for Middleton Manufacturing Company. A work experience student from the local college is with you today. You show him the payments side of the cash book with last week's transactions as follows:

Credit			**Cash Book: Payments**			**CBP 36**
Date	Details	Folio	Discount received	VAT	Cash	Bank
2001			£	£	£	£
1 Oct	Balance b/d					1,588
1 Oct	Teme Traders	PL				585
2 Oct	Insurance	GL				250
2 Oct	Office stationery	GL		14	94	
3 Oct	Tyax Supplies	PL	10			190
4 Oct	Purchases	GL		21		141
4 Oct	Wages	GL			455	
5 Oct	Bank	C			150	
			10	35	699	2,754

You are to explain to the student what each of the transactions represents and the other accounting entries involved in the transactions.

11.4 The following are the payments transactions of Marcle Enterprises for October 2001:

3 Oct	Cash purchases paid for by cheque, £440 + VAT
5 Oct	Paid Jarvis Supplies a cheque for £625 in full settlement of a debt of £645
8 Oct	Bought office equipment, paying by cheque £320 + VAT
9 Oct	Transferred £500 from cash to the bank
12 Oct	Paid Hallam Limited £237 by cheque
16 Oct	Paid salaries by cheque, £2,247 (no VAT)
18 Oct	Paid telephone expenses by cheque, £329 (including VAT)
22 Oct	Paid T Woods a cheque for £439 in full settlement of a debt of £449
24 Oct	Cash purchases paid for by cheque, £400 + VAT
26 Oct	Paid wages in cash, £420 (no VAT)
29 Oct	The owner of the business withdraws £500 by cheque for own use
30 Oct	Cash purchases paid for in cash, £120 + VAT
31 Oct	Withdrew £300 in cash from the bank for use in the business

The rate of Value Added Tax is 17.5%.

Account numbers are to be used – see below.

You are to:

- Enter the above payments on page 67 of the three column cash book of Marcle Enterprises.
- Sub-total the money columns at 31 October.
- Show the entries to be made in the following accounts:

purchases (creditors) ledger

Hallam Limited (account no 455)

Jarvis Supplies (account no 525)

T Woods (account no 760)

general (main) ledger

discount received account (account no 6502)

drawings account (account no 7005)

office equipment account (account no 750)

purchases account (account no 5001)

telephone expenses account (account no 6212)

VAT account (account no 2200)

wages and salaries account (account no 7750)

11.5 The following are the payments transactions of Kendrick and Company for November 2001:

5 Nov	Cash purchases paid for by cheque, £235 (including VAT)
7 Nov	Bought office stationery £40 + VAT, paying in cash
9 Nov	Paid a cheque for £355 to Abel and Company, a creditor, in full settlement of an invoice for £370
12 Nov	Cash purchases for £141 (including VAT) paid in cash
13 Nov	Bought office equipment, paying by cheque, £360 + VAT
15 Nov	Paid an invoice for £250 from A Palmer, a creditor, by cheque for £235, £15 being received for prompt settlement
16 Nov	Loan repayment of £250 made to HSCB Bank by direct debit (no VAT)
19 Nov	The owners of the business withdraw £400 by cheque for own use
21 Nov	Cash purchases of £94 (including VAT) paid in cash
23 Nov	Withdrew £300 in cash from the bank for use in the business
26 Nov	Paid a cheque for £325 to P Singh Limited, a creditor, in full settlement of an invoice for £335
27 Nov	Paid salaries by cheque, £1,552 (no VAT)
28 Nov	Cash purchases of £240 + VAT, paid by cheque
29 Nov	Paid wages in cash, £475 (no VAT)
29 Nov	Paid a cheque for £340 to Abel and Company, a creditor, in full settlement of an invoice for £350
30 Nov	Bought office stationery £120 + VAT, paying by cheque

The rate of Value Added Tax is 17.5%
Account numbers are to be used – see below.

You are to:

- Enter the above payments on page 24 of the cash book of Kendrick and Company, using columns for date, details, discount received, VAT, cash and bank.
- Sub-total the money columns at 30 November.
- Show the entries to be made in the following accounts:

purchases (creditors) ledger

Abel and Company (account no 105)
A Palmer (account no 495)
P Singh Limited (account no 645)

general (main) ledger

discount received account (account no 6502)
drawings account (account no 7005)
loan account: HSBC Bank (account no 2250)
office equipment account (account no 750)
office stationery account (account no 6384)
purchases account (account no 5001)
VAT account (account no 2200)
wages and salaries account (account no 7750)

11.6 Martin Peters runs a building supplies company. He buys in bulk from manufacturers and sells in smaller quantities to trade customers on credit and to the public on cash terms. His business is registered for VAT.

He uses a cash book which analyses payments between:

- discount received
- VAT
- purchases
- purchases (creditors) ledger
- sundry

The following transactions take place during the week commencing 19 November 2001:

19 Nov	Cash purchases of £150.00 (including VAT) paid by cheque
19 Nov	Paid an invoice for £292.65 from Broughton Brick Company (a creditor) by cheque for £286.40 and receiving £6.25 discount for prompt settlement
20 Nov	Paid for stationery in cash, £45.50 (including VAT)
22 Nov	Withdrew £200 in cash from the bank for use in the business
22 Nov	Paid wages £782.31 in cash (no VAT)
22 Nov	Bought shop fittings £395.00 + VAT, paying by cheque
23 Nov	Cash purchases of £80.00 (including VAT) paid for in cash
23 Nov	Paid salaries by cheque, £1,357.00 (no VAT)
23 Nov	Paid an invoice for £468.25 from Wyvern Cement Company (a creditor) by cheque for £458.25 and receiving £10.00 discount for prompt settlement
23 Nov	Paid for stationery by cheque, £85.25 + VAT
23 Nov	Martin Peters withdraws £200.00 in cash from the business for his own use

The rate of Value Added Tax is 17.5%

Account numbers are to be used – see below

You are to:

- Enter the above payments on page 45 of the analysed cash book of Martin Peters (VAT amounts should be rounded down to the nearest penny).
- Sub-total the money columns at 23 November.
- Show the entries to be made in the following accounts:

purchases (creditors) ledger

Broughton Brick Company (account no 125)

Wyvern Cement Company (account no 920)

general (main) ledger

discount received account (account no 6502)

drawings account (account no 7005)

purchases account (account no 5001)

shop fittings account (account no 740)

stationery account (account no 6382)

VAT account (account no 2200)

wages and salaries account (account no 7750)

12 PETTY CASH BOOK

12.1 A company operates its petty cash book using the imprest system. The imprest amount is £250.00. At the end of a particular period the analysis columns are totalled to give the following amounts:

VAT £13.42; postages £29.18; travel £45.47; stationery £33.29; sundry £18.54

How much cash will be required to restore the imprest amount for the next period?

12.2 You work as an accounts assistant in the offices of Hi-Tech Engineering Company, a VAT-registered business. One of your responsibilities is to maintain the petty cash records and you are authorised to approve petty cash vouchers up to a value of £20 each. How will you deal with the following discrepancies and queries?

- A petty cash voucher for stationery is submitted to you for £12.50; the till receipt from the stationery shop shows a total of £10.00
- A petty cash voucher for travelling expenses is submitted to you for £25.50; a rail ticket for this value is attached.
- The total of the analysis columns of the petty cash book is different from the total payments column.
- A colleague asks about the imprest amount and where you keep the keys to the petty cash box.

12.3 You work in the accounts office of Wyvern Printers plc, a company which specialises in printing colour supplements for newspapers. Your supervisor is the main cashier. One of your tasks includes responsibility for all aspects of petty cash.

The accounting procedures manual of Wyvern Printers includes the following references to petty cash:

- A petty cash book is to be maintained using the imprest system.
- The imprest amount at the beginning of each week is to be £250.
- The maximum amount which can be drawn from petty cash is £50 in any one transaction.
- The petty cashier can authorise petty cash vouchers up to £25 for any one transaction; amounts above £25 and up to £50 can be authorised by the main cashier.
- All petty cash transactions must be recorded on petty cash vouchers which are to be
  - numbered in sequence
  - accompanied by relevant supporting documentation
- Authorised petty cash vouchers are to be recorded in a petty cash book with analysis columns for Value Added Tax, Postages, Travel, Stationery, Sundries.

In addition you know that petty cash claims include VAT at the current rate of 17.5%, except for postages, rail and bus travel, newspapers and magazines which are either zero-rated or exempt from VAT.

During the week commencing 15 January 2001 several petty cash vouchers, together with supporting documentation, are passed to you by members of staff. The petty cash vouchers are shown on this and the next page, and the supporting documentation on the two pages following (pages 75 and 76).

You are to:

- refer to the petty cash vouchers and supporting documentation and, for each claim you are satisfied with, you are to sign in the 'authorised' section; the authorised vouchers are to be numbered in sequence beginning with the number 352
- for any petty cash claims you are unable to process, you are to write a memorandum to the main cashier explaining the reasons
- write up the petty cash book for the week commencing 15 January 2001 starting with an imprest balance of £250, and recording the petty cash vouchers that you have authorised
- total the columns and prepare a posting sheet which shows the entries to be recorded in the general (main) ledger at the end of the week, on 19 January (account numbers need not be shown)

Vouchers for the week beginning 15 January 2001 (continued on the next page)

petty cash voucher number ____
date *15 Jan 2001*

description	amount £	p
Travel	*16*	*50*
	16	*50*

signature *J. Jones*
authorised ____

petty cash voucher number ____
date *15 Jan 2001*

description	amount £	p
Meal allowance	*6*	*11*
	6	*11*

signature *J. Jones*
authorised ____

petty cash voucher number ____
date *15 Jan 2001*

description	amount £	p
Stationery	*8*	*46*
	8	*46*

signature *R. Singh*
authorised ____

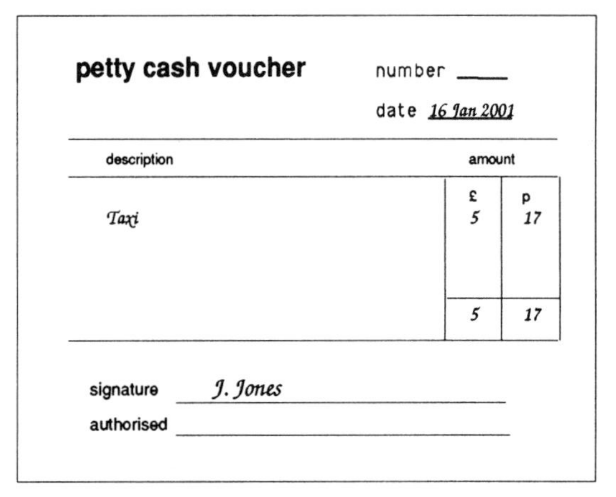

petty cash voucher number ____
date *16 Jan 2001*

description	amount £	p
Taxi	*5*	*17*
	5	*17*

signature *J. Jones*
authorised ____

petty cash voucher number ____
date *16 Jan 2001*

description	amount £	p
Stationery	4	70
	4	70

signature *J. Jones*
authorised ____

petty cash voucher number ____
date *16 Jan 2001*

description	amount £	p
Travel	13	50
	13	50

signature *M. Gono*
authorised ____

petty cash voucher number ____
date *17 Jan 2001*

description	amount £	p
Postages	17	00
	17	00

signature *J. Jones*
authorised ____

petty cash voucher number ____
date *17 Jan 2001*

description	amount £	p
Travel	22	85
	22	85

signature *J. Jones*
authorised ____

petty cash voucher number ____
date *18 Jan 2001*

description	amount £	p
Meal allowance	6	11
	6	11

signature *R. Singh*
authorised ____

petty cash voucher number ____
date *18 Jan 2001*

description	amount £	p
Taxi fare	4	70
	4	70

signature *J. Jones*
authorised ____

petty cash voucher number ____
date *18 Jan 2001*

description	amount £	p
Stationery	14	10
	14	10

signature *J. Jones*
authorised ____

petty cash voucher number ____
date *19 Jan 2001*

description	amount £	p
Postages	25	25
	25	25

signature *M. Gono*
authorised ____

Western Trains plc
PO Box 731, Weston WS1 1QQ
RECEIPT FOR RAIL TICKETS

Amount £ *16.50*
Date *15 Jan 2001*
Issued by *H Vaz*

Western Trains – working towards excellence

Wyvern Printers plc
MEAL ALLOWANCE

Date *15/1/01*
Name *J. JONES*
Amount £ *6.11*
Authorised by *L. Luz, Manager*
Department code *08*

Stationery Suppliers Limited
8 High Street, Wyvern WV1 2AP
VAT registration: 491 7681 20

15 01 2001

Goods	7.20
VAT	1.26
Total	8.46
Tendered	10.00
Change	1.54

Please call again!

Crown Taxis
20 Lime Street, Wyvern WV3 1DS
Telephone: 01901 436941

Date *16/1/01*
Received with thanks £ *5.17*

VAT registration: 495 7681 21

Stationery Suppliers Limited
8 High Street, Wyvern WV1 2AP
VAT registration: 491 7681 20

16 01 2001

Goods	4.00
VAT	0.70
Total	4.70
Tendered	10.00
Change	5.30

Please call again!

Western Trains plc
PO Box 731, Weston WS1 1QQ
RECEIPT FOR RAIL TICKETS

Amount £ *13.50*
Date *17/01/01*
Issued by *J. Clark*

Western Trains – working towards excellence

POST OFFICE COUNTERS LTD
WYVERN HIGH STREET POSTSHOP
VAT REG 647240004 BRANCH NO 0096

15/01/2001 1027

Parcel post

Total to pay	17.00
Cash tendered	20.00
Change	3.00

DON'T FORGET VALENTINE'S DAY!
14th FEBRUARY

Western Trains plc
PO Box 731, Weston WS1 1QQ
RECEIPT FOR RAIL TICKETS

Amount £ *22.85*
Date *17 Jan 2001*
Issued by *H Vaz*

Western Trains – working towards excellence

Wyvern Printers plc
MEAL ALLOWANCE

Date *18 Jan 2001*
Name *R. SINGH*
Amount £ *6.11*
Authorised by *A. Eden, Manager*
Department code *12*

Crown Taxis
20 Lime Street, Wyvern WV3 1DS
Telephone: 01901 436941

Date *18 Jan 2001*
Received with thanks £ *4.70*

VAT registration: 495 7681 21

Stationery Suppliers Limited
8 High Street, Wyvern WV1 2AP
VAT registration: 491 7681 20

18 01 2001

Goods	12.00
VAT	2.10
Total	14.10
Tendered	20.00
Change	6.90

Please call again!

POST OFFICE COUNTERS LTD
WYVERN HIGH STREET POSTSHOP
VAT REG 647240004 BRANCH NO 0096

19/01/2001 1536

Stamps

Total to pay	25.25
Cash tendered	30.00
Change	4.75

DON'T FORGET VALENTINE'S DAY!
14th FEBRUARY

13 FURTHER ASPECTS OF DOUBLE-ENTRY ACCOUNTS

13.1 Tom Griffiths set up in business on 1 March 2001 and registered for Value Added Tax. During the first month he has kept a cash book but, unfortunately, has made some errors:

Debit		**Cash Book: Receipts**			**CBR**
Date	Details	Folio	Discount allowed	Cash	Bank
2001			£	£	£
4 Mar	Office equipment*				1,175
12 Mar	Drawings			125	

Credit		**Cash Book: Payments**			**CBP**
Date	Details	Folio	Discount received	Cash	Bank
2001			£	£	£
3 Mar	Capital				6,500
5 Mar	Bank loan				2,500
7 Mar	Wages				250
10 Mar	Commission received*			141	
12 Mar	Rent paid				200
17 Mar	Van*				7.050

The items with asterisks (*) include Value Added Tax

Tom Griffiths has not got around to the other double-entry accounts.

You are to rewrite the cash book of Tom Griffiths, putting right his errors, and to draw up the other accounts, making the appropriate entries.

Notes:

- Use the current rate of Value Added Tax (17.5 % at the time of writing)
- Account numbers need not be used
- Separate primary accounting records need not be shown

13.2 Enter the following transactions into the double-entry book-keeping accounts of Caroline Yates, who is registered for Value Added Tax:

2001	
3 Nov	Started in business with capital of £75,000 in the bank
4 Nov	Bought a photocopier for £2,400 + VAT, paying by cheque
7 Nov	Received a bank loan of £70,000
10 Nov	Bought office premises £130,000, paying by cheque
12 Nov	Paid rates of £3,000, by cheque
14 Nov	Bought office fittings £1,520 + VAT, paying by cheque
17 Nov	Received commission of £400 + VAT, in cash
18 Nov	Drawings in cash £125
20 Nov	Paid wages £250, by cheque
24 Nov	Paid £100 of cash into the bank
25 Nov	Returned some of the office fittings (unsuitable) and received a refund cheque for £200 + VAT
28 Nov	Received commission £200 + VAT, by cheque

Notes:

- Use the current rate of Value Added Tax (17.5% at the time of writing)
- Account numbers need not be used
- Separate primary accounting records need not be shown

13.3 A friend of yours, Natasha Williams, runs a catering business which supplies food and drink to companies for special events. You keep the 'books' of the business which is registered for VAT.

Natasha tells you about a customer, Mereford Marketing, for whom she provided tea and coffee for their stand at the 'Two Counties Spring Show'. Despite sending monthly statements of account and 'chaser' letters she has still not been paid, and has recently heard that they have gone out of business. It is now 18 December 2001 and Natasha doesn't think she will be able to collect the amount due and asks you to write off the account as a bad debt.

You look up the account in the sales (debtors) ledger:

Dr		**Mereford Marketing**			Cr
2001		£	2001		£
25 Apr	Sales	141			

Natasha reminds you that, as VAT was charged on the original invoice, VAT can be reclaimed when writing off that debt.

You are to:

- show the journal entry made on 18 December 2001
- the transactions on Mereford Marketing's account in the sales (debtors) ledger
- the bad debts written off account in the general (main) ledger
- the VAT account in the general (main) ledger

Note: account numbers need not be used

13.4 You are an accounts assistant at Osborne Electronics. A work experience student from the local college is with you today. You decide to show him several non-routine transactions which are going through the accounts today, the last day of the financial year:

- office equipment has been bought for £1,200 + VAT and paid for by cheque
- the owner of the business has paid in additional capital, £2,500 by cheque (no VAT)
- stock has been valued at £11,350
- the account of a debtor, Tintern Travel, with a balance of £188 is to be written off as a bad debt (VAT-relief is available)

You are to:

(a) Explain to the student what each transaction represents and the double-entry book-keeping involved

(b) Prepare a posting sheet for the transactions under today's date (account numbers need not be used).

16 BALANCING ACCOUNTS AND THE TRIAL BALANCE

16.1 The following are the business transactions of Robert Jefferson, a bookshop owner, for the months of January and February 2001:

Transactions for January

2001	
1 Jan	Started in business with capital of £5,000 in the bank
2 Jan	Paid rent on premises £200, by cheque
3 Jan	Bought shop fittings £2,000, by cheque
6 Jan	Bought stock of books £2,500, on credit from Northam Publishers
8 Jan	Book sales £1,200, paid into bank
9 Jan	Book sales £1,000, paid into bank
13 Jan	Bought books £5,000, on credit from Broadheath Books
15 Jan	Book sales £1,500 to Teme School, a cheque being received
17 Jan	Book sales, £1,250, paid into bank
20 Jan	Bought books from Financial Publications £2,500, by cheque
23 Jan	Teme School returned unsuitable books £580, cheque refund sent
30 Jan	Sold books on credit to Wyvern College, £1,095

Transactions for February

2001	
3 Feb	Book sales £2,510, paid into bank
5 Feb	Paid rent on premises £200, by cheque
7 Feb	Bought shop fittings £1,385, by cheque
10 Feb	Book sales £3,875, paid into bank
11 Feb	Sent cheque, £2,500, to Northam Publishers
13 Feb	Bought books £1,290, on credit from Northam Publishers
14 Feb	Sent cheque, £5,000, to Broadheath Books

17 Feb	Book sales £1,745, paid into bank
18 Feb	Wyvern College returned books, £250
21 Feb	Book sales £1,435, paid into bank
24 Feb	Bought books £1,250, on credit from Associated Publishers
28 Feb	Book sales £3,900, paid into bank

You are to:

(a) Record the January transactions in his double-entry accounts. Balance all the accounts that have more than one transaction at 31 January 2001

(b) Draw up a trial balance at 31 January 2001

(c) Record the February transactions in his double-entry accounts. Balance all the accounts that have more than one transaction at 28 February 2001

(d) Draw up a trial balance at 28 February 2001

Notes:

- *day books are not required*
- *Robert Jefferson is not registered for VAT*

16.2 Kevin Kemp works in the accounts department of a manufacturing company that produces specialist engineering components for the car industry. The company, Turner & Sons Limited, Unit 10, Valley Road Industrial Estate, Mereford, MR1 5PQ, has just computerised its accounting system.

The accountant, Tom Worth, has instructed Kevin that for the first few months, while the accounts are being produced by computer, he is to keep separate manual records of the company's transactions. Kevin's instructions are to record only the documents issued and received; the accountant will record manually cash and bank transactions.

The computer accounting system was introduced on 1 March 2001. At that date, Turner & Sons Limited had the following accounts in the purchases and sales ledgers:

Purchases (creditors) ledger

Ace Forgings Limited, balance	£550.00 credit
Round Tubes Limited, balance	£610.00 credit
Bright Metal Company Limited, balance	£120.00 credit

Sales (debtors) ledger

Toyisson Motors plc, balance	£870.00 debit
Portland Vehicles Limited, balance	£940.00 debit
Bramhall Vehicles plc, balance	£340.00 debit

Turner & Sons Limited had the following balances in the general (main) ledger on 1 March 2001:

- purchases £4,050.00 debit
- sales £9,600.00 credit
- Value Added Tax £832.50 credit

During the first month that the computer was operational (March 2001), Kevin recorded the invoices issued and received shown on pages 83 to 92.

You are to assume the role of Kevin (or Karen) Kemp and undertake the following tasks:

(a) Enter the invoices in the sales day book and purchases day book (as appropriate), and, at the end of March, total the books.

(b) Open the accounts in Turner & Sons Limited's ledger system with the balance on 1 March 2001. Record the accounting entries from the primary accounting records into the appropriate account in Turner & Sons Limited's sales ledger, purchases ledger and general ledger. The accounts needed are:

- Sales (debtors) Ledger – accounts for each customer
- Purchases (creditors) Ledger – accounts for each supplier
- General (main) Ledger – sales account, purchases account, VAT account

(c) Balance each account at 31 March 2001.

(d) Assuming that no money settlement has been forwarded or received during March 2001:

- draw up and complete statements of account for Turner & Sons Limited's customers
- compile a list of the outstanding balances Turner & Sons Limited owes its suppliers
- compile a list of the outstanding balances Turner & Sons Limited is owed by its customers

Note: account numbers need not be shown in the accounting records

No. 1011

INVOICE

TURNER & SONS LTD
Unit 10
Valley Road Industrial Estate
MEREFORD
MR1 5PQ

Tel/Fax: 01605 732491
VAT Reg No 407 8693 82

To:

Toyisson Motors plc
Star Way
RIPTON
RP4 7JH

Date/Tax Point: 3 Mar 2001

Customer Order No. 5871/91

Customer Account No. T 0141

Quantity	Description	Unit Price £	p	Total Amount £	p
20	Mouldings: type ABC123	10	00	200	00
			Total Goods	200	00
			Value Added Tax	35	00
			Total Due	235	00

Terms: Net Monthly
E & OE

No. 1012

INVOICE

TURNER & SONS LTD
Unit 10
Valley Road Industrial Estate
MEREFORD
MR1 5PQ

Tel/Fax: 01605 732491
VAT Reg No 407 8693 82

To:

Bramhall Vehicles plc
140-144 Bramley Way
HALLTOWN
HL2 8AH

Date/Tax Point: 4 Mar 2001

Customer Order No. 27469/01

Customer Account No. B 0103

Quantity	Description	Unit Price £	p	Total Amount £	p
250	Mouldings: type BV861	2	00	500	00
	Total Goods			500	00
	Value Added Tax			87	50
	Total Due			587	50

Terms: Net Monthly
E & OE

INVOICE

Ace Forgings Ltd

Ace Works Tipton Way
PUDLEY PY3 8TD

Tel/Fax: 01681 234966
VAT Reg No 684 9143 21

Invoice to

TURNER & SONS LTD
Unit 10
Valley Road Industrial Estate
MEREFORD MR1 5PQ

Invoice no: 87
Account: 428
Date/tax point: 6 Mar 2001
Order no: TS 6851

Quantity	Description	Unit Price £	p	Total Amount £	p
200 metres	Steel section: type 457	4	00	800	00
	Total Goods			800	00
	Value Added Tax			140	00
	Total Due			940	00

TERMS

NET MONTHLY

CARRIAGE PAID

E & OE

INVOICE

Round Tubes Ltd

The Tube Works
Terry Hill Industrial Estate
BARLASTON PY3 1AJ

Tel/Fax: 01681 794238
VAT Reg No 986 3217 64

Invoice to

TURNER & SONS LTD
Unit 10
Valley Road Industrial Estate
MEREFORD MR1 5PQ

Invoice no: 101
Account: TU 317
Date/tax point: 7 Mar 2001
Order no: TS 6852

Quantity	Description	Unit Price £	p	Total Amount £	p
100 lengths	Plate steel tube: type OJ/157	3	00	300	00
	Total Goods			300	00
	Value Added Tax			52	50
	Total Due			352	50

TERMS

NET MONTHLY

CARRIAGE PAID

E & OE

No. 1013

INVOICE

TURNER & SONS LTD
Unit 10
Valley Road Industrial Estate
MEREFORD
MR1 5PQ

Tel/Fax: 01605 732491
VAT Reg No 407 8693 82

To:

Bramhall Vehicles plc
140-144 Bramley Way
HALLTOWN
HL2 8AH

Date/Tax Point: 10 Mar 2001
Customer Order No. 27521/01
Customer Account No. B 0103

Quantity	Description	Unit Price £ p	Total Amount £ p
50	Gear units: type 747/21	20 00	1,000 00
		Total Goods	1,000 00
		Value Added Tax	175 00
		Total Due	1,175 00

Terms: Net Monthly
E & OE

No. 1014

INVOICE

TURNER & SONS LTD
Unit 10
Valley Road Industrial Estate
MEREFORD
MR1 5PQ

Tel/Fax: 01605 732491
VAT Reg No 407 8693 82

To:

Portland Vehicles Ltd
Portland Works
BRIDGTON
BR4 1AP

Date/Tax Point: 18 Mar 2001

Customer Order No. 386/17

Customer Account No. P 0170

Quantity	Description	Unit Price £	p	Total Amount £	p
75	Gear units: type 747/25	20	00	1,500	00
	Total Goods			1,500	00
	Value Added Tax			262	50
	Total Due			1,762	50

Terms: Net Monthly
E & OE

No. 1015

INVOICE

TURNER & SONS LTD
Unit 10
Valley Road Industrial Estate
MEREFORD
MR1 5PQ

Tel/Fax: 01605 732491
VAT Reg No 407 8693 82

To:

Toyisson Motors plc
Star Way
RIPTON
RP4 7JH

Date/Tax Point: 25 Mar 2001

Customer Order No. 6010/91

Customer Account No. T 0141

Quantity	Description	Unit Price £ p	Total Amount £ p
120	Mouldings: type ABC123	10 00	1,200 00
		Total Goods	1,200 00
		Value Added Tax	210 00
		Total Due	1,410 00

Terms: Net Monthly
E & OE

Invoice no. 58

BRIGHT METAL COMPANY LTD

Unit 91, Cotheridge Industrial Estate
CARPMINSTER CA3 4JT

Tel/Fax: 01724 683910
VAT Reg No: 226 4932 71

Invoice to

TURNER & SONS LTD
Unit 10
Valley Road Industrial Estate
MEREFORD MR1 5PQ

Account: 4271
Date/tax point: 14 Mar 2001
Order no: TS 6853

Quantity	Description	Unit Price £	p	Total Amount £	p
200	Plated pressings: type 6/09	3	00	600	00
	Total Goods			600	00
	Value Added Tax			105	00
	Total Due			705	00

TERMS

NET MONTHLY

CARRIAGE PAID

E & OE

INVOICE

Ace Forgings Ltd

Ace Works Tipton Way
PUDLEY PY3 8TD

Tel/Fax: 01681 234966
VAT Reg No 684 9143 21

Invoice to

TURNER & SONS LTD
Unit 10
Valley Road Industrial Estate
MEREFORD MR1 5PQ

Invoice no: 96
Account: 428
Date/tax point: 25 Mar 2001
Order no: TS 6854

Quantity	Description	Unit Price £	p	Total Amount £	p
100 metres	Steel section: type 457	4	00	400	00
	Total Goods			400	00
	Value Added Tax			70	00
	Total Due			470	00

TERMS

NET MONTHLY
CARRIAGE PAID
E & OE

INVOICE

Round Tubes Ltd

The Tube Works
Terry Hill Industrial Estate
BARLASTON PY3 1AJ

Tel/Fax: 01681 794238
VAT Reg No 986 3217 64

Invoice to

TURNER & SONS LTD
Unit 10
Valley Road Industrial Estate
MEREFORD MR1 5PQ

Invoice no: 109
Account: TU 317
Date/tax point: 31 Mar 2001
Order no: TS 6855

Quantity	Description	Unit Price £	Unit Price p	Total Amount £	Total Amount p
70 lengths	Steel tube: type OP/191	2	00	140	00
	Total Goods			140	00
	Value Added Tax			24	50
	Total Due			164	50

TERMS

NET MONTHLY

CARRIAGE PAID

E & OE

16.3 The following account appears in your firm's purchases (creditors) ledger:

Dr		**William Shaw**			Cr
2001		£	2001		£
10 Mar	Purchases returns	156	1 Mar	Balance b/d	640
12 Mar	Bank	624	4 Mar	Purchases	756
	Discount	16	20 Mar	Purchases	845
25 Mar	Purchases returns	45			
30 Mar	Bank	780			
	Discount	20			

During the first week of April, the following statement of account was received from William Shaw:

date	details	debit	credit	balance
2001		£	£	£
1 Mar	Balance b/d			640
2 Mar	Invoice 2841	756		1,396
10 Mar	Credit note 347		156	1,240
14 Mar	Payment received		624	
	Discount allowed		16	600
18 Mar	Invoice 3017	845		1,445
25 Mar	Credit note 357		45	1,400
29 Mar	Invoice 3278	1,027		2,427

You are to:

- Balance the account of William Shaw in your purchases ledger at 31 March 2001
- Reconcile the balance on your purchases ledger account at 31 March 2001 with that shown on the statement

16.4 The bank columns of Jane Doyle's cash book for May 2001 are as follows:

2001	*Receipts*	£	2001	*Payments*		£
1 May	Balance b/d	300	2 May	P Stone	867714	28
7 May	Cash	162	14 May	Alpha Ltd	867715	50
16 May	C Brewster	89	29 May	E Deakin	867716	110
23 May	Cash	60				
30 May	Cash	40				

She received her bank statement which showed the following transactions for May 2001:

BANK STATEMENT		Payments	Receipts	Balance
2001		£	£	£
1 May	Balance brought forward			300 CR
5 May	Cheque no 867714	28		272 CR
7 May	Credit		162	434 CR
16 May	Standing order: A-Z Insurance	25		409 CR
19 May	Credit		89	498 CR
20 May	Cheque no. 867715	50		448 CR
26 May	Credit		60	508 CR
31 May	Bank Charges	10		498 CR

You are to:

(a) check the items on the bank statement against the items in the cash book and update the cash book accordingly; total the cash book and clearly show the balance carried down

(b) give *two* reasons why the balance in the cash book does not match the closing balance on the bank statement

16.5 You work as a trainee in the office of Speciality Paints Limited, a company which buys special types of paints and other finishes from the manufacturers and sells them in your area to local businesses. This week the cashier, who is responsible for keeping the company's cash book is away on holiday. You have been asked to carry out her work for the week commencing 8 September 2001.

At the start of the week the cash book has a balance at bank of £802.50, and cash in hand of £120.68. The following are the transactions to be entered in the cash book for the week:

Cheques received from debtors

8 Sep £389.51 from Wyvern County Council, in full settlement of an invoice for £398.01

10 Sep £451.20 from J Jones & Company

12 Sep £458.25 from Building Supplies Limited, in full settlement of an invoice for £468.25

Note: all cheques received are banked on the day of receipt.

Cheques drawn

8 Sep Cheque no. 123451 for £263.49, payee ITI Paint Division Limited, a creditor, in full settlement of an invoice for £269.24

9 Sep Cheque no. 123452 for £100.00, payee Cash (the cash was drawn for use in the business)

9 Sep Cheque no. 123453 for £169.75, payee United Telecom plc

10 Sep Cheque no. 123454 for £394.20, payee Wages

11 Sep Cheque no. 123455 for £160.38, payee Paint Manufacturing plc, in full settlement of an invoice for £163.88

Cash received from debtors

9 Sep	£27.50 from T Lewis

12 Sep	£22.91 from H Simms, in full settlement of an invoice for £23.41

Cash paid

11 Sep	£88.50 for casual labour

At the end of the week, the bank statement shown below is received.

You are to:

- Enter the transactions for the week in the three-column (with columns for discount, cash, bank) cash book of Speciality Paints Limited.
- Check the bank statement and write the cash book (bank columns) up-to-date with any items appearing on the bank statement that need to be recorded in the cash book.
- Balance the cash book at 12 September 2001, and show the discount accounts as they will appear in the firm's general (main) ledger.
- Give *four* reasons why the balance in the cash book (bank columns) does not match the closing balance on the bank statement.
- Write a memorandum to the office manager regarding any matter that you consider should be queried with the bank. Use the blank memorandum printed on page 94.

National Bank PLC

Branch Mereford

Account Speciality Paints Ltd

Account number 12345678 **Statement number** 45 **date** 12 Sep 2001

Date	Details	Payments	Receipts	Balance
2001		£	£	£
8 Sep	Balance brought forward			802.50 Cr
8 Sep	Credit		389.51 ✓	1,192.01 Cr
9 Sep	Cheque 123452	100.00 ✓		1,092.01 Cr
9 Sep	DD Wyvern Hire Purchase	85.50 ✓		1,006.51 Cr
10 Sep	Cheque 123454	394.20 ✓		612.31 Cr
10 Sep	Credit		451.20 ✓	1,063.51 Cr
10 Sep	BGC Johnson & Co		125.50	1,189.01 Cr
11 Sep	Cheque 123451	263.49 ✓		925.52 Cr
11 Sep	Cheque 874111	25.00		900.52 Cr
12 Sep	Bank charges	12.50		888.02 Cr

SO Standing Order **DD** Direct Debit **TR** Transfer **BGC** Bank giro credit **BACS** Automated transfer

MEMORANDUM

To

From

Date

Subject

16.6 The cashier where you work as an accounts assistant has asked you to balance the petty cash book for the week ending 16 May 2001. The petty cash book is kept on the imprest system and, at the end of each week, cash is withdrawn from the main cash book to restore the imprest amount to £100.00.

The petty cash book is as follows:

Receipts	Date	Details	Voucher No	Total Payment	Analysis columns				
					VAT	Postages	Travel	Meals	Stationery
£ p	2001			£ p	£ p	£ p	£ p	£ p	£ p
100.00	12 May	Balance b/d							
	12 May	Travel	461	6.50			6.50		
	13 May	Meal allowance	462	6.11				6.11	
	13 May	Stationery	463	8.46	1.26				7.20
	13 May	Taxi	464	5.17	0.77		4.40		
	14 May	Stationery	465	4.70	0.70				4.00
	14 May	Travel	466	3.50			3.50		
	14 May	Postages	467	4.50		4.50			
	15 May	Bus fares	468	3.80			3.80		
	15 May	Catering	469	10.81	1.61			9.20	
	16 May	Postages	470	3.50		3.50			
	16 May	Stationery	471	7.52	1.12				6.40
	16 May	Travel	472	6.45			6.45		

You are to:

- restore the imprest amount of petty cash book to £100.00, making the appropriate entry (note: the main cash book entry for this transaction need not be shown)
- balance the petty cash book at 16 May 2001, bringing down the balance on 17 May

16.7 The book-keeper of Lorna Fox has extracted the following list of balances as at 31 March 2001:

	£
Purchases	96,250
Sales	146,390
Sales returns	8,500
Administration expenses	10,240
Wages	28,980
Telephone	3,020
Interest paid	2,350
Travel expenses	1,045
Premises	125,000
Machinery	30,000
Stock at 1 Jan 2001	8,240
Debtors	12,150
Bank overdraft	1,050
Cash	150
Creditors	9,619
Value Added Tax (credit balance)	2,876
Loan from bank	20,000
Drawings	9,450
Capital	155,440

You are to:

(a) Produce the trial balance at 31 March 2001.

(b) Take any three debit balances and any three credit balances and explain to a trainee who has just started work with the accounts department why they are listed as such, and what this means to the business.

16.8 Fill in the missing words from the following sentences:

(a) "You made an error of .... when you debited the cost of diesel fuel for the van to Vans Account."

(b) "I've had the book-keeper from D Jones Limited on the 'phone concerning the statements of account that we sent out the other day. She says that there is a sales invoice charged that she knows nothing about. I wonder if we have done a .... and it should be for T Jones' account?"

(c) "There is a 'bad figure' on a purchases invoice – we have read it as £35 when it should be £55. It has gone through our accounts wrongly so we have an error of .... to put right."

(d) "Although the trial balance balanced last week, I've since found an error of £100 in the calculation of the balance of sales account. We will need to check the other balances as I think we may have a .... error."

(e) "Who was in charge of that trainee last week? He has entered the payment for the electricity bill on the debit side of the bank and on the credit side of electricity – a .... of ...."

(f) "I found this purchase invoice from last week in amongst the copy letters. As we haven't put it through the accounts we have an error of ...."

16.9 A friend, who is just beginning her studies of book-keeping comments:

- "if the trial balance totals agree it is proof that the book-keeping entries are 100 per cent correct"
- "I wouldn't know where to start looking if the trial balance totals did not agree."

What would you reply to your friend?

17 CONTROL ACCOUNTS

17.1 Would the following errors cause a difference between the balance of the sales (debtors) ledger control account and the total of the balances in the sales (debtors) ledger?

(a) The sales day book was overcast by £100.

(b) The amount of a sales invoice was debited to the account of Wyvern Traders instead of Wyvern Tiling.

(c) An invoice for £54 was recorded in the sales day book as £45.

17.2 Mereford Manufacturing Company Limited maintains a sales ledger (debtors) control account in its general (main) ledger as part of its double-entry system. Individual accounts for customers are kept on a memorandum basis in a separate subsidiary sales ledger.

On 1 November 2001 the sales ledger contains the following accounts:

A Abercrombie	balance £643.29 debit
Burton and Company	balance £1,472.41 debit
H Haig	balance £462.28 debit
T Norton	balance £392.48 debit
Shipley Limited	balance £68.87 debit
Yarnold and Sons Limited	balance £976.18 debit

The following transactions, which have been authorised by the accounts supervisor, took place during November:

4 Nov	Sold goods on credit to A Abercrombie £225 + VAT, and T Norton £380 + VAT
5 Nov	H Haig settled his account in full by cheque
7 Nov	T Norton returned goods £151 + VAT
11 Nov	Yarnold and Sons Limited settled an invoice for £292.65 by cheque after deducting £6.25 cash discount
13 Nov	Sold goods on credit to Burton and Company £775 + VAT, and T Norton £195 + VAT
14 Nov	A Abercrombie returns goods £45 + VAT
17 Nov	Sold goods on credit to Yarnold and Sons Limited £458 + VAT
18 Nov	A Abercrombie settles her account in full by cheque after deducting £16.27 cash discount
21 Nov	Transferred the balance of T Norton's account to his account in the purchases (creditors) ledger

25 Nov	Sold goods on credit to A Abercrombie £495 + VAT, and T Norton £169 + VAT
28 Nov	Wrote off the account of Shipley Limited as a bad debt

You are to:

(a) write up the personal accounts in the sales (debtors) ledger of Mereford Manufacturing for November 2001, balancing them at the end of the month

(b) prepare a sales ledger (debtors) control account for November 2001, balancing it at the end of the month

(c) reconcile the control account balance with the debtors' accounts at 1 November and 30 November 2001

Note: Mereford Manufacturing Company is registered for VAT; day books are not required.

17.3 Mereford Manufacturing Company Limited maintains a purchases ledger (creditors) control account in its general (main) ledger as part of its double-entry system. Individual accounts for suppliers are kept on a memorandum basis in a separate subsidiary purchases ledger.

On 1 November 2001 the purchases ledger contains the following accounts:

Bakewell Limited	balance £476.81 credit
Don Edge and Company	balance £1,107.52 credit
M Lister	balance £908.04 credit
T Norton	balance £543.21 credit
Percival and Company	balance £250.49 credit
Trent Supplies plc	balance £749.25 credit
Vector Metals Limited	balance £397.64 credit

The following transactions, which have been authorised by the accounts supervisor took place during November:

5 Nov	Bought goods on credit from Trent Supplies £179 + VAT, and Percival and Company £352 + VAT
7 Nov	Paid the balance of M Lister's account by cheque after deducting £15.34 cash discount
10 Nov	Bought goods on credit from T Norton £450 + VAT, and Vector Metals £370 + VAT
14 Nov	Paid by cheque an invoice from Don Edge and Company for £585.30 after deducting £12.50 cash discount
17 Nov	Returned goods to Percival and Company £28 + VAT
19 Nov	Bought goods on credit from Bakewell Limited £255 + VAT, and M Lister £302 + VAT
20 Nov	Paid Vector Metals Limited a cheque for the balance of the account
21 Nov	Transfer of debit balance of £890.68 in the sales (debtors) ledger to T Norton's account in the purchases (creditors) ledger
26 Nov	Returned goods to Vector Metals Limited £68 + VAT

You are to:

(a) write up the personal accounts in the purchases (creditors) ledger of Mereford Manufacturing for November 2001, balancing them at the end of the month

(b) prepare a purchases ledger (creditors) control account for November 2001, balancing it at the end of the month

(c) reconcile the control account balance with the creditors' accounts at 1 November and 30 November 2001

Note: Mereford Manufacturing Company is registered for VAT; day books are not required.

17.4 Stourminster Limited uses control accounts for its purchases ledger and sales ledger. At 1 September 2001 the balances of the control accounts were:

	Debit	*Credit*
	£	£
Purchases ledger	128	65,027
Sales ledger	106,943	558

The following transactions took place during September 2001:

	£
Credit purchases	137,248
Credit sales	179,984
Sales returns	2,081
Purchases returns	6,349
Cash/cheques received from customers	163,481
Cash/cheques paid to suppliers	125,636
Customers' cheques dishonoured	357
Discount allowed	2,549
Discount received	1,832
Bad debts written off	528
Transfer of a credit balance from the purchases ledger to the sales ledger	2,086

At 30 September 2001, there were debit balances in the purchases ledger of £479 and credit balances in the sales ledger of £694

You are to:

- prepare the purchases ledger (creditors) control account and sales ledger (debtors) control account of Stourminster Limited for September 2001
- balance the accounts at 30 September 2001

17.5 You work as an accounts assistant for The Stationery Box, a retailer of office stationery and supplies.

One of the items stocked by The Stationery Box is photocopying paper – this is packed in boxes, each containing five reams (a ream = 500 sheets of paper). The accounts supervisor tells you a physical stock take of photocopying paper was carried out today: it showed that there were 350 boxes in stock, at a cost of £10 each, giving a stock valuation of £3,500. The stocktaker also noted that there were two damaged boxes – these were not included in the stock take as they were unsaleable and should be thrown away.

The Accounts Supervisor gives you the stock record card (below) and asks you to complete it and to make a reconciliation with the physical stock at 30 June 2001. If there is an imbalance, make a note to the accounts supervisor suggesting where you think the difference may have occurred.

STOCK RECORD

Product: photocopying paper
Stock units: boxes

Date	Details	In	Out	Quantity in stock	Value at £10 per box
2001					£
1 Jun	Opening balance			300	3,000
4 Jun	Receipt	100		400	4,000
5 Jun	Issued		30	370	3,700
6 Jun	Issued		20	350	3,500
8 Jun	Issued		25		
11Jun	Issued		40		
13 Jun	Receipt	100			
15 Jun	Issued		35		
18 Jun	Issued		24		
19 Jun	Receipt	100			
20 Jun	Issued		32		
22 Jun	Issued		28		
25 Jun	Issued		42		
27 Jun	Issued		35		
28 Jun	Receipt	100			
29 Jun	Issued		37		

RECONCILIATION OF STOCK TAKE AND STOCK RECORD AS AT 30 JUNE 2001

	£
Physical stock take	....
Stock record card balance	....
Difference	....

Note to Accounts Supervisor:

18 THE JOURNAL AND CORRECTION OF ERRORS

18.1 The purchase of £20 of stationery has been debited to office equipment account. This is:

(a) an error of original entry

(b) an error of principle

(c) a mispost/error of commission

(d) a reversal of entries

Answer (a) or (b) or (c) or (d)

18.2 A credit purchase of £63 from T Billington has been entered in the accounts as £36. This is:

(a) a reversal of entries

(b) an error of original entry

(c) a compensating error

(d) an error of omission

Answer (a) or (b) or (c) or (d)

18.3 Telephone expenses of £250 paid by cheque have been debited to the bank columns of the cash book and credited to the telephone expenses account. Which of the following entries will correct the error?

	Debit		*Credit*	
(a)	Bank	£250	Telephone expenses	£250
(b)	Telephone expenses	£250	Bank	£250
(c)	Bank	£250	Telephone expenses	£250
	Bank	£250	Telephone expenses	£250
(d)	Telephone expenses	£250	Bank	£250
	Telephone expenses	£250	Bank	£250

Answer (a) or (b) or (c) or (d)

18.4 The following list of balances was taken from the accounting records of Len Lewis on 31 August 2001:

	£
Office equipment	18.750
Stock	4,525
Debtors	10,294
Creditors	8,731
Bank overdraft	879
Cash	354
VAT (credit balance)	1,396
Capital	25,000
Drawings	15,391
Sales	175,686
Purchases	97.243
Sales returns	3,604
Purchases returns	2,856
General expenses	64,387

On 3 September 2001 the following errors and omissions were discovered:

- a sales invoice for £400 + VAT had not been entered in the sales day book
- a cheque for £625 from a debtor had not been recorded in the accounts
- Len Lewis had taken drawings of £300 by cheque but no entries had been made in the accounts
- a purchases invoice for £200 + VAT had been entered twice in the purchases day book

You are to: prepare a trial balance for Len Lewis' business at 31 August 2001 after adjusting for the above errors and omissions.

18.5 You have recently taken over writing up the double-entry accounts of B Brick (Builders). You have found a number of errors made by the previous book-keeper as follows:

(a) Credit purchase of goods for £85 from J Stone has not been entered in the accounts

(b) A cheque for £155 received from Roger Williams, a debtor, has been credited to the account of another debtor, William Rogers

(c) Diesel fuel costing £30 has been debited to vehicles account

(d) A credit sale for £154 to T Potter has been entered in the accounts as £145

(e) The total of purchases returns day book has been overcast by £100 as has wages account

You are to take each error in turn and:

- state the type of error
- show the correcting journal entry

Note: VAT is to be ignored; use today's date for the journal entries.

18.6 Tracey Truslove is the book-keeper for Mereford Traders Limited. At 30 June 2001 she is unable to balance the trial balance. The difference, £149 credit, is placed to a suspense account pending further investigation.

The following errors are later found:

(a) Purchases account is undercast by £100.

(b) A cheque for £95 for the purchase of stationery has been recorded in the stationery account as £59.

(c) Rent received of £205 has been debited to both the rent received account and the bank account.

(d) Vehicles expenses of £125 have not been entered in the expenses account.

You are to:

- make journal entries to correct the errors
- show the suspense account after the errors have been corrected

Note: VAT is to be ignored; the corrections are to be made on 9 July 2001.

19 USING THE TRIAL BALANCE

The following background information is common to both Student Activities in this section:

You work as an accounts assistant for 'Hotspot Barbecues'. The company manufactures barbecues and accessories, and sells them to garden centres, country shops, and direct to the public. Hotspot Barbecues is registered for VAT.

Your job in the accounts department is principally concerned with the main (general) ledger and the individual accounts of debtors and creditors, which are kept in subsidiary ledgers as memorandum accounts.

19.1 Today is 1 August 2001 and you are working on the main (general) ledger and subsidiary (purchases) ledger sections of the accounting system.

Transactions

The following transactions all occurred on 1 August 2001 and have been entered into the relevant primary accounting records (given below). No entries have yet been made into the ledger system. VAT has been calculated at the rate of 17.5%.

PURCHASES DAY BOOK

Date 2001	*Details*	*Invoice No*	*Total £*	*VAT £*	*Net £*
1 Aug	Reade Manufacturing	794	1,175	175	1,000
1 Aug	Reed Supplies Ltd	201	1,645	245	1,400
1 Aug	Bourne Limited	387	1,880	280	1,600
1 Aug	Eveshore Services	924	2,350	350	2,000
	Totals		7,050	1,050	6,000

PURCHASES RETURNS DAY BOOK

Date 2001	*Details*	*Credit Note No*	*Total £*	*VAT £*	*Net £*
1 Aug	Eveshore Services	CN 68	235	35	200
1 Aug	Reed Supplies Ltd	CN 32	517	77	440
	Totals		752	112	640

CASH BOOK

Date 2001	*Details*	*Discount Allowed*	*Bank £*	*Date 2001*	*Details*	*Discount Received*	*Bank £*
1 Aug	Balance b/d		4,200	1 Aug	Bourne Limited		2,500
1 Aug	Rent received		500	1 Aug	Reade Manufacturing	75	2,925
1 Aug	Balance c/d		770	1 Aug	Bank charges		45
			5,470			75	5,470

Balances to be inserted in ledger accounts

The following balances are relevant to you at the start of the day on 1 August 2001:

	£
Creditors:	
Bourne Limited	3,840
Eveshore Services	2,330
Reade Manufacturing	3,000
Reed Supplies Limited	4,970
Purchases	197,384
Purchases returns	2,590
Creditors control	32,860
Discount received	710
Rent received	3,250
Rates paid	1,930
Bank charges	335
VAT (credit balance)	3,980

Journal entries

The following errors have been discovered and will need to be entered into the journal and double-entry accounts:

- a credit purchase of £550 made on 24 July 2001 from Reade Manufacturing has been recorded in the account of Reed Supplies Limited
- an amount of £375 for rates paid was debited to rent received account in error on 17 July 2001

Balances to be transferred to trial balance

	£
Premises	125,000
Machinery	30,000
Vehicles	28,200
Stock	15,590
Cash	200
Debtors control	55,390
Capital	120,000
Sales	376,332
Sales returns	3,640
Discount allowed	845
Wages and salaries	68,140
Electricity	5,260
Bad debts written off	434
Vehicle expenses	3,174

Task 1.1 Enter the opening balances listed on the previous page (106) into the following accounts which are provided on the next three pages (108 - 110):

Bourne Limited
Eveshore Services
Reade Manufacturing
Reed Supplies Limited
Purchases
Purchases returns
Creditors control
Discount received
Rent received
Rates paid
Bank charges
VAT

Task 1.2 From the day books and cash book shown on pages 105 and 106 make the relevant entries into the accounts in the subsidiary (purchases) ledger and the main (general) ledger.

Task 1.3 Record the entries in the journal (narratives are not required) shown on page 111 to correct the two errors and then enter the transactions into the relevant accounts.

Task 1.4 Balance off all of the accounts at 1 August 2001 *showing clearly the balances carried down.*

Task 1.5 Transfer the balances calculated in task 1.4, and from the cash book, to the relevant columns of the trial balance shown on page 112.

Task 1.6 Transfer the remaining balances shown at the top of this page to the trial balance and total each column. The debit column and credit column totals should be the same.

Tasks 1.1, 1.2, 1.3 and 1.4

SUBSIDIARY (PURCHASES) LEDGER

Bourne Limited

Date	Details	Amount £	Date	Details	Amount £

Eveshore Services

Date	Details	Amount £	Date	Details	Amount £

Reade Manufacturing

Date	Details	Amount £	Date	Details	Amount £

Reed Supplies Limited

Date	Details	Amount £	Date	Details	Amount £

MAIN (GENERAL) LEDGER

Purchases

Date	Details	Amount £	Date	Details	Amount £

Purchases returns

Date	Details	Amount £	Date	Details	Amount £

Creditors control

Date	Details	Amount £	Date	Details	Amount £

Discount received

Date	Details	Amount £	Date	Details	Amount £

MAIN (GENERAL) LEDGER

Rent received

Date	Details	Amount £	Date	Details	Amount £

Rates paid

Date	Details	Amount £	Date	Details	Amount £

Bank charges

Date	Details	Amount £	Date	Details	Amount £

VAT

Date	Details	Amount £	Date	Details	Amount £

JOURNAL

Date	*Details*	*Debit*	*Credit*

Tasks 1.5 and 1.6

TRIAL BALANCE AS AT 1 AUGUST 2001

	Debit	Credit
	£	£
Premises	....	....
Machinery	....	....
Vehicles	....	....
Stock	....	....
Bank	....	....
Cash	....	....
Debtors control	....	....
Capital	....	....
Sales	....	....
Sales returns	....	....
Discount allowed	....	....
Wages and salaries	....	....
Electricity	....	....
Bad debts written off	....	....
Vehicle expenses	....	....
Purchases	....	....
Purchases returns	....	....
Creditors control	....	....
Discount received	....	....
Rent received	....	....
Rates paid	....	....
Bank charges	....	....
VAT	....	....
TOTAL		

19.2 Today is 2 August 2001 and you are working on the main (general) ledger and subsidiary (sales) ledger sections of the accounting system.

Transactions

The following transactions all occurred on 2 August 2001 and have been entered into the relevant primary accounting records (given below). No entries have yet been made into the ledger system. VAT has been calculated at the rate of 17.5%.

SALES DAY BOOK

Date 2001	*Details*	*Invoice No*	*Total £*	*VAT £*	*Net £*
2 Aug	Charlton Home Furnishings	504	940	140	800
2 Aug	Tauntone Country Store	505	1,175	175	1,000
2 Aug	A-Z Garden Centre	506	1,410	210	1,200
2 Aug	Charlton Home Furnishings	507	470	70	400
	Totals		3,995	595	3,400

SALES RETURNS DAY BOOK

Date 2001	*Details*	*Credit Note No*	*Total £*	*VAT £*	*Net £*
2 Aug	A-Z Garden Centre	CN 63	188	28	160
2 Aug	Tauntone Country Store	CN 64	329	49	280
	Totals		517	77	440

CASH BOOK

Date 2001	*Details*	*Discount Allowed*	*Bank £*	*Date 2001*	*Details*	*Discount Received*	*Bank £*
2 Aug	Charlton Home			2 Aug	Balance b/d		770
	Furnishings	60	2,340	2 Aug	Wages and salaries		3,227
2 Aug	A-Z Garden Centre		1,000				
2 Aug	Balance c/d		657				
		60	3,997				3,997
					Balance b/d		657

Balances to be inserted in ledger accounts

The following balances are relevant to you at the start of the day on 2 August 2001:

	£
Debtors:	
A-Z Garden Centre	1,268
Charlton Home Furnishings	2,400
Ralph's Gardens	141
Tauntone Country Store	797
Sales	376,332
Sales returns	3,640
Debtors control	55,390
Discount allowed	845
Vehicles	28,200
Vehicle expenses	3,174
Wages and salaries	68,140
VAT (credit balance)	3,042
Bad debts written off	434

Journal entries

The accounts supervisor asks you to make entries in the journal and the double-entry accounts for the following:

- the subsidiary (sales) ledger account balance in the name of Ralph's Gardens is to be written off as a bad debt; you are told that VAT relief is available on this debt
- an amount of £200 + VAT for vehicle expenses was debited to vehicles account in error on 26 July 2001

Balances to be transferred to trial balance

	£
Premises	125,000
Machinery	30,000
Stock	15,590
Cash	200
Creditors control	33,658
Capital	120,000
Purchases	203,384
Purchases returns	3,230
Discount received	785
Rent received	4,125
Electricity	5,260
Rates paid	2,305
Bank charges	380

Task 2.1 Enter the opening balances listed on the previous page (114) into the following accounts which are provided on the next three pages (116 - 118):

A-Z Garden Centre

Charlton Home Furnishings

Ralph's Gardens

Tauntone Country Store

Sales

Sales returns

Debtors control

Discount allowed

Vehicles

Vehicle expenses

Wages and salaries

VAT

Bad debts written off

Task 2.2 From the day books and cash book shown on page 113 make the relevant entries into the accounts in the subsidiary (sales) ledger and the main (general) ledger.

Task 2.3 Record the entries in the journal (narratives are not required) shown on page 119 for the two adjustments required by the accounts supervisor, and then enter the transactions into the relevant accounts.

Task 2.4 Balance off all of the accounts at 2 August 2001 showing clearly the balances carried down.

Task 2.5 Transfer the balances calculated in task 2.4, and from the cash book, to the relevant columns of the trial balance shown on page 120.

Task 2.6 Transfer the remaining balances shown at the bottom of page 114 to the trial balance and total each column. The debit column and credit column totals should be the same.

Tasks 2.1, 2.2, 2.3 and 2.4

SUBSIDIARY (PURCHASES) LEDGER

A-Z Garden Centre

Date	*Details*	*Amount* £	*Date*	*Details*	*Amount* £

Charlton Home Furnishings

Date	*Details*	*Amount* £	*Date*	*Details*	*Amount* £

Ralph's Gardens

Date	*Details*	*Amount* £	*Date*	*Details*	*Amount* £

Tauntone Country Store

Date	*Details*	*Amount* £	*Date*	*Details*	*Amount* £

MAIN (GENERAL) LEDGER

Sales

Date	Details	Amount £	Date	Details	Amount £

Sales returns

Date	Details	Amount £	Date	Details	Amount £

Debtors control

Date	Details	Amount £	Date	Details	Amount £

Discount allowed

Date	Details	Amount £	Date	Details	Amount £

MAIN (GENERAL) LEDGER

Vehicles

Date	*Details*	*Amount* £	*Date*	*Details*	*Amount* £

Vehicle expenses

Date	*Details*	*Amount* £	*Date*	*Details*	*Amount* £

Wages and salaries

Date	*Details*	*Amount* £	*Date*	*Details*	*Amount* £

VAT

Date	*Details*	*Amount* £	*Date*	*Details*	*Amount* £

Bad debts written off

Date	Details	Amount £	Date	Details	Amount £
2/8	Balance b/d	434		Balance c/d	554
2/8	Ralph's Gardens	120			
		554			554
	Balance b/d	554			

JOURNAL

Date	Details	Debit	Credit
2/8	Bad debts written off account	120	
	VAT a/c	21	
	Ralph's Gardens		141
2/8	Vehicles a/c		200
	Vehicle expenses	200	

Tasks 2.5 and 2.6

TRIAL BALANCE AS AT 1 AUGUST 2001

	Debit	Credit
	£	£
Premises	....	....
Machinery	....	....
Vehicles	....	....
Stock	....	....
Bank	....	....
Cash	....	....
Debtors control	....	....
Capital	....	....
Sales	....	....
Sales returns	....	....
Discount allowed	....	....
Wages and salaries	....	....
Electricity	....	....
Bad debts written off	....	....
Vehicle expenses	....	....
Purchases	....	....
Purchases returns	....	....
Creditors control	....	....
Discount received	....	....
Rent received	....	....
Rates paid	....	....
Bank charges	....	....
VAT	....	....
TOTAL		

20 INFORMATION FOR MANAGEMENT CONTROL

20.1 In the first list below, five items of information are shown, labelled A to E. These are examples of the kind of information which managers of a business might find useful. In the second list below, six possible management tasks are shown, labelled (i) to (vi).

For each of the six management tasks, list the items of information from the first list, A to E, which managers may find useful for that task. There may be more than one item for each task and the items may be used more than once.

- A Rates of pay for different grades of labour
- B Sales forecasts for a product for the next year at different selling prices
- C The total cost of repairs to machinery in the last year
- D Estimated prices of raw materials for the next year
- E The amount of time lost during the last year due to machine breakdowns

- (i) Deciding on selling prices for products in the future
- (ii) Budgeting for the cost of production for the next year
- (iii) Checking monthly totals of wages
- (iv) Deciding whether to scrap old machines and buy new ones
- (v) Preparing a budget for the next quarter, to make sure sufficient cash is available when needed
- (vi) Finding ways to reduce costs within the business.

20.2 For each of the management tasks (i) to (vi) in Activity 20.1 (above), state which of the following functions of management would best describe that task:

Decision-making

Planning

Control

20.3 Which of the phrases below describe features of financial accounting and which describe features of management accounting?

- (a) reports relating to what has happened in the past
- (b) may be required by law
- (c) gives estimates of costs and income for the future
- (d) may be made public
- (e) gives up-to-date reports which can be used for controlling the business
- (f) is used by people outside the business

(g) is designed to meet requirements of people inside the business

(h) shows details of the costs of materials, labour and expenses

(i) records accurate amounts, not estimates

20.4 A friend of yours, Rob Willis, started his own business several years ago, making small toys from moulded plastics. The business has expanded rapidly and now employs 8 production workers, 4 people in selling and distribution and 3 office workers. A book-keeper records all the business transactions and, at the end of the financial year, the financial accounts are prepared by an accountant. Up to now, Rob Willis has managed the business fairly successfully, making decisions on a day-to-day basis. So that he can improve his management skills he asks your advice about making use of management accounting information.

Write a note to Rob Willis explaining how management accounting differs from financial accounting, and suggesting ways in which management accounting information might help him in managing his business.

20.5 The following are items of expenditure incurred in a company which manufactures clothing. Write them in three columns, headed 'Materials costs', 'Labour costs' and 'Expenses'.

(a) Premium for the insurance of buildings

(b) Salaries of the office staff

(c) The cost of zip fasteners

(d) The cost of electricity

(e) Wages of storekeepers

(f) Overtime payments for machinists

(g) The cost of a consignment of blue denim

(h) The cost of preprinted stationery

(i) The cost of television advertising

(j) The cost of cones of thread

(k) Road fund licences for vehicles

(l) The canteen chef's wages

20.6 Suggest likely cost centres or profit centres for each of the following:

A theatre in a provincial town, where touring productions are staged. The theatre has a bar and a confectionery counter. Ticket sales are dealt with by the theatre's own box office, and the plays are advertised locally.

A garage, which sells both new and used cars of two different makes. Cars are also repaired, serviced and valeted.

20.7 You work for Gold and Partners, Chartered Accountants, who have three offices in neighbouring districts in the suburbs of London. The Senior Partner, Lawrence Gold, sent the following memo to your line manager, Marie McCall. You have been asked to extract and prepare the information requested in the memo. The offices are referred to as R, S and T. They are all of similar size.

MEMORANDUM

To: M. McCall

From: L. Gold

Date: 26 October 2000

Subject: Annual Review: year ended 30.9.00

I am in the process of reviewing the firm's figures for the year ended 30 September and require the following:

- Income totals for each of the three offices.
- Costs for each of the three offices, broken down into materials, labour and expenses.
- Profit and Return on Investment calculated for each office separately.

Please supply these as soon as possible.

You extract the following information from the records:

Income for the year ended 30 September 2000:
Office R: £950,000
Office S: £869,000
Office T: £1,195,500

Materials costs for the year ended 30 September 2000:
Office R: £75,000
Office S: £7,000
Office T: £8,400

Labour costs for the year ended 30 September 2000:
Office R: £650,000
Office S: £550,000
Office T: £730,000

Expenses for the year ended 30 September 2000:
Office R: £82,500
Office S: £69,000
Office T: £89,100

The amount of money invested in each office at 30 September 2000 is as follows:
Office R: £750,000
Office S: £900,000
Office T: £1,150,000

Which of these amounts appears to be incorrect and should be queried with Marie McCall?

Marie McCall investigates your query and agrees that an error has been made. The correct figure is £7,500, which you should use. She suggests that you write out of all the above information in columns, with one column for the narrative and one for each Office (see the format below). When you have calculated the profit for each office and the return on investment, these can also be entered in the columns, in order to present the information clearly for Lawrence Gold.

	Office R (£)	Office S (£)	Office T (£)
Materials			
Labour			
Expenses			
TOTAL COSTS			
Income			
PROFIT			
Money invested			
Return on Investment (%)			

20.8 In your summer holiday, you are doing some voluntary work in the office of a charity. The charity raises money through Members' Subscriptions, Shops, Street Collections and Donations and a Christmas Mail Order Catalogue. Much of the work done for the charity is unpaid, but there is a certain amount of paid work in essential administration. There are also some costs of materials and expenses which are not donated. The Christmas Mail Order has costs similar to businesses. The chief administrator of the charity has asked you to draw up a table, as follows:

YEAR ENDED 31.12.2000	Street Collections and Donations (£)	Shops (£)	Christmas Mail Order (£)	Members' Subscriptions (£)
Materials				
Labour				
Expenses				
TOTAL COSTS				
Income				
Surplus of Income over total costs (see Note 1)				
Surplus as a percentage of Income (Note 2)				

Note 1: Surplus = Income – total costs, similar to profit for a business

Note 2: To calculate the surplus as a percentage of income, the formula is:

$$\frac{SURPLUS}{INCOME} \times 100\%$$

You then extract the following information for the year from the records and complete the table.

Christmas Mail Order

Income from sales was £375,300.

Costs were: materials £260,000, labour £46,000, expenses £13,000

Street Collections and Donations

Income was £12,650.

Costs were: materials £2,500, labour £3,000, expenses £1,800

Shops

Income was £78,600.

Costs were: materials £8,300, labour £21,000, expenses £5,700

Members' Subscriptions

Income was £11,200

Costs were: Materials £900, labour £3,000, expenses £1,800.

20.9 In your everyday life there are almost certainly a number of coding systems which you use, or systems which apply codes to you personally or to your household. For example, the system of Post Codes, which in the UK consist of combinations of letters and numbers. Some coding systems use numbers only and some letters only.

Identify at least *three* coding systems which you use or which are applied to you in your everyday life. State whether the codes are made up of letters or numbers or combinations of both. Provide examples of the codes used within each system.

20.10 The following is an extract from the coding reference manual for a company which processes sugar beet. The sugar which is produced is then packed for distribution.

Extract from list of cost centre codes:

Beet preparation	010
Processing	020
Packing	030
Administration	040
Quality control	050
Distribution	060

Extract from list of expenditure codes:

Sugar beet	1010
Stationery	1050
Machine operators' wages	2010
Supervisory wages	2040
Drivers' wages	2050
Heating and lighting	3020
Power for machinery	3030
Telephone	3040

Each item of expenditure is to be coded with the appropriate cost centre code, followed by the expenditure code, eg Distribution drivers' wages would be coded 060 2050.

Determine the codes for the following in this way (ignore VAT):

(a) Wages paid to machine operators in the processing department

(b) Cost of telephone calls made by the administration department

(c) Cost of electricity used for heating the packing department

(d) Cost of stationery used in the administration department

(e) Wages of the supervisor in the preparation department

(f) Cost of a consignment of beet to be charged to the preparation department

(g) Cost of power used to run the processing machines

(h) Cost of stationery used by the quality control inspectors

21 PRESENTING AND COMPARING MANAGEMENT INFORMATION

21.1 You are working in the accounts department of a company which manufactures electrical goods in several factories and you are passed the following memorandum

> ***MEMORANDUM***
>
> To: Accounts dept.
> From: Production Manager, East Region
> Date: 28 August 2000
> Subject: Costing
>
> I need some information for sending in a report to Head Office, as follows:
>
> - materials costs for last month in the two East Region factories
> - labour costs as above, showing basic and overtime for different grades of production employees.
>
> I need this by the end of the week, please.

List and explain briefly the factors you would have to bear in mind when preparing a reply to this memorandum.

21.2 You have just started work in a small firm which designs and makes curtains to customers' requirements. The curtains are delivered and hung for the clients. You have been asked to sort out some information and present it in a table for the owner, who wants to review how prices are set.

The figures have been jotted down in a notebook by the workshop supervisor, as shown below. Omitting unnecessary text, show the financial information in columns (a column for each job). The costs should be split into Materials, Labour and Expenses. The total cost and the selling price for each job should also be shown.

NOTES

22/8/00 Mrs Johnston:

Measure/design visit (Jane), wages £20;

Lux/Olive Green fabric 22m @ £16.50 per metre and Olive green lining needed 20m @ £7.40 per metre.

Tapes etc £15

Labour: Cutting: 2 hrs at £10 per hr, Making 7 hrs @ £8 per hr

continued on next page

Return visit (Jane and Pete), wages £30.

General expenses £50.

Total cost £702, selling Price £840.

28/8/00 Mr and Mrs Wright:

Measure/design (Paul), wages £20.

Require 10m @ £19.50 per m, (Arcadia check, blue/beige).

Plus 8m @ £18.00 per m, (Arcadia plain blue) and lining 18m @ £7.40 (mid-blue).

Tapes etc £14, Tiebacks (twist, ref 65b) £32.

Labour: Cutting 2 hrs @ £10 per hr, Making 8 hrs @ £8 per hr.

Return visit (Paul and Jane) wages £30.

General expenses, £40.

Total cost £692.20, selling price £830.

31/8/00 Timms and Co (Board Room):

Measure/design visit (Paul), wages £20.

Require 14m @ £27.50 (old gold, ref v131) plus lining 14m @ £7.40 (gold).

Labour: Cutting 1.5 hrs @ £10 per hr, Making 8 hrs @ £8 per hr.

Tapes, pelmet backing, braid (lt. Bronze), etc £38.

Return visit (Pete and Paul), wages £30.

General expenses, £50.

Total cost £705.60, selling price £850.

21.3 Greens Garden Services is a firm which carries out landscaping, grass-cutting and general garden work. You have the following information:

Greens Garden Services: Monthly Income in £.												
Year	Jan	Feb	Mar	Apr	May	June	July	Aug	Sept	Oct	Nov	Dec
2000	900	2100	3000	3000	4200	3300	4350	4200	4200	2100	900	600
2001	300	2400	3250	3750	4100	4200	4500	3600	4000	2000	1500	1500

Prepare a table to show the monthly cumulative totals of Greens Garden Services income for each of the years 2000 and 2001.

21.4 The following forecasts of monthly sales income for the year 2000 were made by the manager of a large public house.

Forecast Sales Income: The Red Lion. Monthly forecast, year 2000												
	Jan	Feb	Mar	Apr	May	June	July	Aug	Sept	Oct	Nov	Dec
£	4000	4000	4500	4500	4500	5000	5000	5500	4500	4000	3500	5000

Actual figures for sales income for the first eight months are now available:

Actual Sales Income: The Red Lion. Monthly Income, year 2000												
	Jan	Feb	Mar	Apr	May	June	July	Aug	Sept	Oct	Nov	Dec
£	3600	3900	4100	4200	4800	5200	4800	5700				

Prepare a table to allow comparison of actual sales income of The Red Lion with the forecast, for corresponding months and for cumulative totals. Complete the table as far as possible.

21.5 You work part-time in the office of a theatre in a city in the west of England. The theatre manager, Kate Leith, has left a note on your desk as follows:

> 3/10/01
>
> From: Kate Leith
>
> ---
>
> Kevin: could you please find out the following for me:
>
> - Total costs for the quarter July-Sept inclusive this year
> - Forecast total cost figure for the same quarter this year
> - Total cost figure for the corresponding quarter last year

You look up the information needed to answer these questions, and find the following table:

Albion Theatre: Quarterly Costs			
All in £000s	**Actual Year 2000**	**Forecast Year 2001**	**Actual Year 2001**
Jan-Mar	135	150	153
Apr-June	151	165	169
July-Sept	144	165	172
Oct-Dec	139	160	

Set out a suitable reply to the note from Kate Leith. What method would you use to give the reply?

21.6 The Albion Theatre costs for the quarter October to December 2001 amount to £156,000. Enter this figure in the table and also fill in the right hand column of differences between the forecast and actual costs for each quarter of 2001. Finally, total each column for the year.

Albion Theatre Quarterly Costs				
All in £000s	**Actual Year 2000**	**Forecast Year 2001**	**Actual Year 2001**	**Forecast – Actual Year 2001**
Jan-Mar	135	150	153	
Apr-June	151	165	169	
July-Sept	144	165	172	
Oct-Dec	139	160		
TOTAL				

21.7 You work in the accounts office of a garage, which has a repairs and servicing department as well as a sales department. You have been asked to complete the following Standard Cost Report:

STANDARD COST REPORT - Fox Motors

Department: Repairs and Servicing

Period: Week commencing 6 Nov 2000

	Forecast Cost (£)	**Actual Cost (£)**	**Discrepancy (£) + or -**
MATERIALS	6,000	5,380	
LABOUR	1,200		
EXPENSES	1,000		
TOTAL			

You have to ask your supervisor for the actual labour and expenses and you are told that these are £1,350 for labour and £875 for expenses.

Complete the report as requested.

21.8 You work as assistant to the management accountant in Floristry Supplies Ltd, a company which sells fresh flowers on a wholesale basis. You are asked to complete as far as possible the following Sales Budgetary Control Report, which has been started by someone else.

SALES BUDGETARY CONTROL REPORT – FLORISTRY SUPPLIES LTD

Date: *August 2000*

	Forecast Sales (monthly) £000s	**Forecast Sales (cumulative) £000s**	**Actual Sales (monthly) £000s**	**Actual–Forecast (monthly) + or – £000s**
January	130	130	126	
February	200	330	211	
March	180	510	169	
April	170		167	
May	150		161	
June	160		164	
July	160		155	
August	150			
September	150			
October	150			
November	160			
December	200			
TOTAL				

You now find out that the actual sales for the month of August 2000 amount to £148,000. Enter this in the report, complete the cumulative forecast sales, and calculate and enter the differences in the right hand column as far as possible. Finally, calculate and enter the appropriate totals.

21.9 You work as assistant to the management accountant in Top Taste Ltd, a company which manufactures a number of brands of biscuits. You are asked to complete the following Product Sales Report, which has been started by someone else.

PRODUCT SALES REPORT – TOP TASTE LTD

Date: *March 2001*

Product Code	Forecast Sales £000s	Actual Sales £000s	Actual–Forecast + or – £000s
B110	55	58	
B123	60	57	
B147	50	52	
C342	25		
C355	25		
C369	30		
C371	30		
D588	45	49	
D590	40	39	
TOTAL			

You have to find out the figures for four of the products. From department C, you obtain the following information:

March 2001 Actual Sales, Department C:

Product Code C342 £27,000

Product Code C355 £24,000

Product Code C369 £28,000

Product Code C371 £33,000

Enter these missing Sales figures in the report and complete the rest of the table.

21.10 In the offices of Top Taste Ltd, there have recently been several problems caused by the unauthorised use of confidential information. You have therefore decided that staff should be reminded about the correct procedures for confidential items. You are planning to put a poster on the wall in each office, showing "The Do's and Don'ts for Confidential Info".

List and explain briefly the main points which you would highlight on the poster.

Unit 1
Practice Simulation

Compuware.com

suggested time 3 hours

SCENARIO

This Simulation is based on Compuware.com Limited, a company which supplies computers, accessories and software to businesses and to the general public. The company sells on credit to its business customers and also operates a shop where the public can make purchases. The tasks in the Simulation include:

- preparation and checking of customer invoices from orders received
- preparation and checking of credit notes in reply to requests for credit
- recording credit transactions in the appropriate accounting records
- preparing statements of account to be sent to customers
- checking cheques, debit/credit card and cash receipts and entering them in the accounting records
- preparing paying-in documents

NVQ UNIT 1 – ELEMENTS COVERED

1 process documents relating to goods and services supplied

2 receive and record receipts

PRACTICE SIMULATION COMPUWARE.COM

unit 1

SITUATION

You work in the Accounts Department of Compuware.com, a company which sells computers, accessories and software to businesses and to the general public. The business is located on a business park. The address is Compuware.com Limited, Unit 14 Monkwood Estate, Witley Green, MR3 6TH.

Your work is varied and involves processing orders received from businesses who buy on credit, dealing with the cheque, credit/debit card and cash receipts which come from sales over the shop counter on the premises, and keeping the accounting records up-to-date.

GOODS SUPPLIED TO CUSTOMERS ON CREDIT

Compuware.com sells on credit to a number of business customers. It gives varying trade discounts to regular customers and offers, on request, a cash discount of 2.5% for settlement of invoices within seven days of issue. An extract from the customer database is shown below.

Compuware.com gives 30 days credit on its invoices and sends out monthly statements of account. It is company policy to chase up invoices which have not been settled in the month following issue – ie in March it will chase up invoices issued in January and earlier.

Compuware.com is registered for VAT and charges VAT at the current rate on all sales.

An extract from the customer database is shown below.

Compuware.com Customer database (extract)

customer details	account no.	trade discount	credit limit £	balance £ (1 June 2001)
Harpney Ltd 12 Gretarex Road, Chelnor, MR1 6YT	3412	10%	10,000	8,560.00
Brinkman & Co Unit 2 Freshwater Estate, Grantley, GR4 6FG	3520	15%	25,000	18,960.50
King Designs Ltd 45 High Road, Hexworth, HW3 6VB	3340	10%	10,000	3,450.00
D Shaw & Partners Equity House, The Square, Pithwick, PW2 7FG	3401	20%	40,000	25,500.60
Star Insurance Brokers 7 Broad Street, Mereford, MR1 7CF	3521	15%	30,000	19,600.80
Hellrose Associates 8 The Terrace, Malpeck, HR6 8HG	3470	10%	10,000	12,750.80

COUNTER SALES

Compuware.com operates a retail shop at its premises and sells to members of the public on a cash basis – ie it accepts cash, cheques and debit/credit card payments. There are two EFTPOS tills in use. At the end of each day the debit card and credit card payment totals are automatically sent via computer link to Compuware's bank account. The total of the cash and cheque receipts are recorded by the senior cashier on a Receipts Summary which is used by you on a daily basis to prepare a bank paying-in slip.

BANKING DETAILS

Compuware.com has a business account with Western Bank Plc at its Witley Green branch.

PRODUCTS

Compuware.com sells a wide range of computers, accessories and software. An extract from its catalogue is shown below.

Compuware.com Product catalogue (extract)

code	product	unit	price £ (excluding VAT)
101008	Zap3 desktop computer	each	650.00
101009	Zap4 desktop computer	each	750.00
101010	Zap5 desktop computer	each	950.00
101020	Mercury laptop computer	each	1,150.00
101045	Digiviz digital camera	each	695.00
102007	Zap65 CD writer	each	495.00
103007	Zap CD diskpack (10 CDs in a box)	box	49.50
103008	Zap DVD diskpack (10 DVDs in a box)	box	65.50
150101	Macrohard 'The Business' software	each	400.00
150102	Adept 'Photomake' software	each	450.00
150109	Querk 'Page Manager' software	each	600.00

ACCOUNTING RECORDS

Compuware.com records sales invoices in a sales day book, and credit notes issued in a sales returns day book. A manual system of double-entry book-keeping is used, with a cash book and a main (general) ledger. The main ledger includes a control account for debtors, with customer accounts contained in a subsidiary (sales) ledger.

TASKS

PART 1: DEALING WITH CREDIT SALES

1. Refer to the six purchase orders on pages 138 to 140, the price list on page 135 and the customer details on page 134.

   Two of the purchase orders will need referring to Ivor Pound, your Supervisor. Decide which purchase orders these are and write a memo (see page 141) to your supervisor explaining the problem.

   The date is 4 June 2001

2. Complete the four sales invoices on pages 142 to 145.

   Remember to apply the correct trade discount in all cases and allow cash discount when it is requested by a customer.

   VAT is chargeable at the current rate on all sales.

   The date is 4 June 2001

3. Enter the four sales invoices from task 2 into the sales day book on page 157.

   Total the sales day book and record the accounting entries in the main (general) ledger and subsidiary (sales) ledger accounts on pages 158 to 160. Note: opening balances are shown on these accounts where appropriate.

4. On 12 June 2001 you receive the three requests for credit shown on page 146 – two e-mails and a returns note.

   You investigate the delivery to D Shaw and Partners and find that the goods were delivered to the correct address of D Shaw and Partners on 6 June. Your carrier (Puma Parcels) faxes you a copy of the delivery note signed by a Mr B Speers who accepted the parcel on 6 June.

   You refer the matter to your supervisor Ivor Pound and he asks you to:

   (a) complete the two credit notes (on pages 147-148) for Star Insurance and King Designs

   (b) draft a letter to D Shaw and Partners (page 149) for Mr Pound's signature explaining that credit cannot be given at present because the goods have been delivered; the letter should attach a copy of the fax showing the signature of B Speers who accepted the parcel

5. Enter the two sales credit notes from task 4 into the sales returns day book on page 157.

   Total the sales returns day book and record the accounting entries in the main (general) ledger and subsidiary (sales) ledger accounts on pages 158 to 160.

6. In your in-tray on 12 June 2001 are three cheques received from customers in respect of outstanding accounts (see page 150).

   You are to check the cheques for any technical irregularities. One of the cheques will need to be sent back to the customer.

   You are to draft a suitable letter to the customer (see page 151). You can sign the letter in your own name.

7 Record in the cash book (page 159) the two valid cheques received from customers – the cheques were banked on 12 June 2001 – and make the entries in the main (general) ledger and subsidiary (sales) ledger accounts on pages 158 to 160.

8 At the end of the month you prepare statements for your credit customers. Prepare the statements (page 152) for Star Insurance and King Designs and date them 29 June 2001. Use the opening balance shown on the customer database (page 134) and remember to include any payments received.

PART 2: DEALING WITH CASH SALES

The Compuware.com shop has two EFTPOS tills operating during the working day. Both tills accept cash, cheques and debit/credit card payments. At the end of each day the debit card and credit card payment totals are automatically sent via computer link to Compuware's bank account and are recorded on a printout from each till.

At the end of each day, the cashiers Jade Mason and Rashid Singh count up the cash and add up the cheques. The total of the cash, cheques, debit and credit card sales are recorded on a till summary for each till. The amounts that are to be paid into the bank (the cash and cheques) are then transferred to a Bank Summary Sheet which is used as the basis for the preparation of a bank paying-in slip.

9 Complete the two till summaries for 4 June 2001 on pages 153 and 154 from the information given.

10 Complete the Bank Summary Sheet on page 155 from the two till summaries.

11 Complete the bank paying-in slip on page 156. It will be paid in on 5 June 2001. List the cheques on the reverse of the paying-in slip.

12 Enter the amount of the till receipts into the cash book and sales account on pages 158 and 159.

Note: record separate figures in the accounts for the amount banked, debit card receipts, and credit card receipts

ANSWER PAGES

Harpney Limited
12 Gretarex Road
Chelnor
MR1 6YT
01908 672561
VAT REG GB 0745 8383 66

PURCHASE ORDER

Compuware.com Limited
Unit 14 Monkwood Estate
Witley Green
MR3 6TH

purchase order no 355345
date 30 05 01

product code	quantity	description
1001008	1	Zap4 desktop computer @ £750

AUTHORISED signature...date.....................

Brinkman & Co
Unit 2 Freshwater Estate,
Grantley, GR4 6FG
01203 987562
VAT REG GB 0988 8644 12

PURCHASE ORDER

Compuware.com Limited
Unit 14 Monkwood Estate
Witley Green
MR3 6TH

purchase order no 92342
date 29 05 01

product code	quantity	description
1001008	1	Zap3 desktop computer @ £650 Please allow 2.5% cash discount as normal

AUTHORISED signature *D Brinkman* date *29/05/01*

King Designs Limited
45 High Road
Hexworth
HW3 6VB
01804 876293
VAT REG GB 7612 8244 12

PURCHASE ORDER

Compuware.com Limited
Unit 14 Monkwood Estate
Witley Green
MR3 6TH

purchase order no 24342
date 30 05 01

product code	quantity	description
101045	1	Digiviz digital camera @ £695

AUTHORISED signature *A R King* date *30/05/01*

D Shaw & Partners
Equity House
The Square
Pithwick PW2 7FG
01506 775662
VAT REG GB 2357 8644 15

PURCHASE ORDER

Compuware.com Limited
Unit 14 Monkwood Estate
Witley Green
MR3 6TH

purchase order no 2954
date 29 05 01

product code	quantity	description
102007	1	Zap65 CD writer @ £495
103007	1 box of 10	Zap CD diskpack @ £49.50

AUTHORISED signature *B Shaw* date *29/05/01*

Star Insurance Brokers **PURCHASE ORDER**

7 Broad Street
Mereford
MR1 7CF
01908 333391
VAT REG GB 2873 8276 34

Compuware.com Limited
Unit 14 Monkwood Estate
Witley Green
MR3 6TH

purchase order no 2444
date 28 05 01

product code	quantity	description
150109	1	Querk Page Manager @ £600
150102	1	Adept Photomake @ £450
103007	2 boxes	Zap CD diskpack @ £49.50 each

AUTHORISED signature *H Taylor* date *28/05/01*

Hellrose Associates **PURCHASE ORDER**

8, The Terrace
Malpeck
HR6 8HG
01303 542863
VAT REG GB 0911 8633 11

Compuware.com Limited
Unit 14 Monkwood Estate
Witley Green
MR3 6TH

purchase order no 9653
date 29 05 01

product code	quantity	description
1001008	2	Zap3 desktop computers @ £650 each

AUTHORISED signature *J Rose* date *29/05/01*

MEMORANDUM

To

From

Date

Subject

INVOICE

COMPUWARE.COM LIMITED

Unit 14, Monkwood Estate, Witley Green, MR3 6TH
Tel 01908 765311 Fax 01908 765953 Email compuware@goblin.com
VAT Reg GB 0456 1007 19

invoice to

invoice no 10281

account

your reference

date/tax point

product code	description	quantity	price	unit	total	discount %	net

goods total	
VAT	
TOTAL	

terms
Net monthly
Carriage paid
E & OE

INVOICE

COMPUWARE.COM LIMITED

Unit 14, Monkwood Estate, Witley Green, MR3 6TH
Tel 01908 765311 Fax 01908 765953 Email compuware@goblin.com
VAT Reg GB 0456 1007 19

invoice to

invoice no 10282

account

your reference

date/tax point

product code	description	quantity	price	unit	total	discount %	net

terms
Net monthly
Carriage paid
E & OE

goods total	
VAT	
TOTAL	

INVOICE

COMPUWARE.COM LIMITED

Unit 14, Monkwood Estate, Witley Green, MR3 6TH
Tel 01908 765311 Fax 01908 765953 Email compuware@goblin.com
VAT Reg GB 0456 1007 19

invoice to

invoice no 10283

account

your reference

date/tax point

product code	description	quantity	price	unit	total	discount %	net

terms
Net monthly
Carriage paid
E & OE

goods total	
VAT	
TOTAL	

INVOICE

COMPUWARE.COM LIMITED

Unit 14, Monkwood Estate, Witley Green, MR3 6TH
Tel 01908 765311 Fax 01908 765953 Email compuware@goblin.com
VAT Reg GB 0456 1007 19

invoice to

invoice no 10284

account

your reference

date/tax point

product code	description	quantity	price	unit	total	discount %	net

terms
Net monthly
Carriage paid
E & OE

goods total	
VAT	
TOTAL	

REQUESTS FOR CREDIT RECEIVED BY COMPUWARE.COM

To address <compuware@goblin.com>
From: Star Insurance <StarIB@u-net.com>
Subject: Shortages on Delivery
Date: 12.06.01.09.30.34

To Accounts Department

Order Reference 2444

We ordered 2 boxes of CDs on PO 2444 and were invoiced for 2 boxes, but received only one box. Please credit us for shortage. We will re-order next month. Thanks.

Regards

Jane Salter
Accounts Department (Purchases Ledger)

King Designs Limited
45 High Road
Hexworth
HW3 6VB
01804 876293
VAT REG GB 7612 8244 12

RETURNS NOTE

Compuware.com Limited
Unit 14 Monkwood Estate
Witley Green
MR3 6TH

returns note no 1073
date 08 06 01

product code	quantity	description
101045	1	Digiviz digital camera @ £695

REASON FOR RETURN *Faulty goods – please credit in full*

signature *A R King* date *08/06/01*

To address <compuware@goblin.com>
From: D Shaw & Partners <DShawPartners@u-net.com>
Subject: Non delivery of order
Date: 12.06.01.10.34.16

To Accounts Department

Order Reference 2954

On 29 May we ordered (PO ref 2954) 1 x Zap CD writer and a box of 10 CDs. We have received your invoice but not the goods. Please cancel the order and credit in full.

Bertie Shaw
Accounts Department (Purchases Ledger)

CREDIT NOTE

COMPUWARE.COM LIMITED

Unit 14, Monkwood Estate, Witley Green, MR3 6TH
Tel 01908 765311 Fax 01908 765953 Email compuware@goblin.com
VAT Reg GB 0456 1007 19

to

credit note no 1071

account

your reference

our invoice

date/tax point

product code	description	quantity	price	unit	total	discount %	net

reason for credit:

goods total	
VAT	
TOTAL	

CREDIT NOTE

COMPUWARE.COM LIMITED

Unit 14, Monkwood Estate, Witley Green, MR3 6TH
Tel 01908 765311 Fax 01908 765953 Email compuware@goblin.com
VAT Reg GB 0456 1007 19

to

credit note no 1072

account

your reference

our invoice

date/tax point

product code	description	quantity	price	unit	total	discount %	net

reason for credit:

goods total	
VAT	
TOTAL	

COMPUWARE.COM LIMITED

Unit 14, Monkwood Estate, Witley Green, MR3 6TH
Tel 01908 765311 Fax 01908 765953 Email compuware@goblin.com
VAT Reg GB 0456 1007 19

CUSTOMER CHEQUES FOR CHECKING

Albion Bank PLC
7 The Avenue
Broadfield BR1 2AJ

Date *4 June 2001*

90 47 17

Pay *Compuware.com Ltd*

Eight thousand five hundred and sixty pounds only

A/c payee only

£ *8,560.00*

HARPNEY LIMITED

K C Watt *L Richards*

Director Director

083772 90 47 17 11719881

WESTSIDE BANK PLC
22 Cornbury Street
Shelford SL1 2DC

Date

78 37 17

Pay *Compuware.com Limited*

Three thousand four hundred and fifty pounds only

A/c payee only

£ *3,450.00*

KING DESIGNS LIMITED

J King *R Singh*

Director Director

072628 78 37 17 23487611

Britannia Bank PLC
89 High Street
Broadfield BR1 8GH

Date *5 June 2001*

33 44 07

Pay *Compuware.com Limited*

Seven thousand five hundred pounds only

A/c payee only

£ *7,500.00*

BRINKMAN & CO

987482 33 44 07 24221913

COMPUWARE.COM LIMITED

Unit 14, Monkwood Estate, Witley Green, MR3 6TH

Tel 01908 765311 Fax 01908 765953 Email compuware@goblin.com

VAT Reg GB 0456 1007 19

STATEMENT OF ACCOUNT

COMPUWARE.COM LIMITED

Unit 14, Monkwood Estate, Witley Green, MR3 6TH
Tel 01908 765311 Fax 01908 765953 Email compuware@goblin.com
VAT Reg GB 0456 1007 19

TO

account

date

date	details	debit £	credit £	balance £

AMOUNT NOW DUE £

STATEMENT OF ACCOUNT

COMPUWARE.COM LIMITED

Unit 14, Monkwood Estate, Witley Green, MR3 6TH
Tel 01908 765311 Fax 01908 765953 Email compuware@goblin.com
VAT Reg GB 0456 1007 19

TO

account

date

date	details	debit £	credit £	balance £

AMOUNT NOW DUE £

TILL SUMMARY SHEET

Till no 1 Cashier Jade Mason Date 4 June 2001

CASH RECEIVED

Denomination	number	amount (£)
£50 notes	3	
£20 notes	12	
£10 notes	42	
£5 notes	8	
£2 coins	4	
£1 coins	24	
50p coins	16	
20p coins	12	
10p coins	23	
5p coins	7	
2p coins	14	
1p coins	17	
TOTAL CASH		

CHEQUES RECEIVED

Name	amount (£)
J Smith	50.00
R Patel	87.75
K Simmons	45.95
K Burton	45.95

TOTAL CHEQUES	
TOTAL DEBIT CARD RECEIPTS	3,678.90
TOTAL CREDIT CARD RECEIPTS	7,570.50
TOTAL TILL RECEIPTS	

TILL SUMMARY SHEET

Till no 2 Cashier Rashid Singh Date 4 June 2001

CASH RECEIVED

Denomination	number	amount (£)
£50 notes	4	
£20 notes	11	
£10 notes	31	
£5 notes	4	
£2 coins	6	
£1 coins	31	
50p coins	12	
20p coins	11	
10p coins	36	
5p coins	9	
2p coins	20	
1p coins	8	

TOTAL CASH

CHEQUES RECEIVED

Name	amount (£)
R Hazel	49.50
J Nutt	99.60
W Tell	78.50
R Cox	120.50
K Permain	99.95

TOTAL CHEQUES	
TOTAL DEBIT CARD RECEIPTS	1,245.90
TOTAL CREDIT CARD RECEIPTS	5,470.85
TOTAL TILL RECEIPTS	

BANK SUMMARY SHEET

Date 4 June 2001

CASH RECEIVED

Denomination	amount (£)
£50 notes	
£20 notes	
£10 notes	
£5 notes	
£2 coins	
£1 coins	
50p coins	
20p coins	
10p coins	
5p coins	
2p coins	
1p coins	

TOTAL CASH

CHEQUES RECEIVED

	amount (£)
Till 1	
Till 2	

TOTAL CHEQUES

TOTAL BANKED

Date banked ______________________

Summary prepared by ______________________

Date ______________

Cashier's stamp and initials

bank giro credit

Code no	46 76 88
Bank	Western Bank PLC
Branch	Witley Green

Credit: Compuware.com Limited

Account No.: 12034765

Number of cheques

Paid in by ______________

Do not write below this line

£50 notes		
£20 notes		
£10 notes		
£5 notes		
£2/£1		
50p		
20p		
10p,5p		
Bronze		
Total Cash		
Cheques etc		
£		

Details of cheques etc	Amount	
TOTAL CARRIED OVER £		

SALES DAY BOOK

Date	Details	Invoice No	Total £ p	VAT £ p	Net £ p

SALES RETURNS DAY BOOK

Date	Details	Credit Note No	Total £ p	VAT £ p	Net £ p

MAIN (GENERAL) LEDGER

Sales

Date 2001	Details	Amount £ p	Date 2001	Details	Amount £ p
			1 Jun	Balance b/d	224,736.50

Sales returns

Date 2001	Details	Amount £ p	Date 2001	Details	Amount £ p
1 Jun	Balance b/d	7,493.25			

Debtors Control

Date 2001	Details	Amount £ p	Date 2001	Details	Amount £ p
1 Jun	Balance b/d	115,751.50			

Value Added Tax

Date 2001	Details	Amount £ p	Date 2001	Details	Amount £ p
			1 Jun	Balance b/d	8,321.35

Cash Book: Receipts

Date 2001	Details	Discount allowed £ p	Cash £ p	Bank £ p
1 Jun	Balances b/d		115.00	11,207.25

SUBSIDIARY (SALES) LEDGER

Harpney Limited (account no 3412)

Date 2001	Details	Amount £ p	Date 2001	Details	Amount £ p
1 Jun	Balance b/d	8,560.00			

Brinkman Limited (account no 3520)

Date 2001	Details	Amount £ p	Date 2001	Details	Amount £ p
1 Jun	Balance b/d	18,960.50			

King Designs Limited (account no 3340)

Date 2001	*Details*	*Amount* £ p	*Date* 2001	*Details*	*Amount* £ p
1 Jun	Balance b/d	3,450.00			

D Shaw & Partners (account no 3401)

Date 2001	*Details*	*Amount* £ p	*Date* 2001	*Details*	*Amount* £ p
1 Jun	Balance b/d	25,500.60			

Star Insurance Brokers (account no 3521)

Date 2001	*Details*	*Amount* £ p	*Date* 2001	*Details*	*Amount* £ p
1 Jun	Balance b/d	1,960.80			

Hellrose Associates (account no 3470)

Date 2001	*Details*	*Amount* £ p	*Date* 2001	*Details*	*Amount* £ p
1 Jun	Balance b/d	12,750.80			

Unit 2
Practice Simulation

Frontpage Stationery

suggested time 3 hours

SCENARIO

This Simulation is based on Frontpage Stationery, a sole trader stationery wholesale business run by Jessie Page. The business, which has six employees on the payroll, buys in and supplies stationery to a wide range of businesses. The tasks in the Simulation include:

- checking and approval of suppliers' invoices
- checking and approval of suppliers' credit notes
- making payment by cheque and remittance advice on receipt of suppliers' statements
- paying employees on the payroll and making the PAYE payment to the Inland Revenue
- keeping accounting records up-to-date
- making petty cash payments

NVQ UNIT 2 – ELEMENTS COVERED

1. process documents relating to goods and services received
2. prepare authorised payments
3. receive and record payments

PRACTICE SIMULATION FRONTPAGE STATIONERY

SITUATION

You work as book-keeper for Jessie Page who runs a sole trader wholesale stationery business – Frontpage Stationery – in Knightwick. The business operates from Unit 2 Hillside Trading Estate, Knightwick, MR6 7LP. She employs six staff. She sells by mail order and also from a showroom in the Unit. Her customers are mainly businesses, but she also supplies stationery to schools and colleges. She runs a stationery stall at the local College each September.

Your work involves writing up the accounting records and running the payroll (both of which are done manually). You have to check suppliers' invoices, despatch notes, credit notes, and statements to ensure that you pay for what you have received, and on the right terms.

You are responsible for running the weekly payroll and for making the monthly PAYE payment to the Inland Revenue. Employees are paid through the Albion Bank 'Auto Credit' BACS payment system.

You are also responsible for a petty cash system which is run on a day-to-day basis by Jessie.

Jessie Page is registered for VAT.

GOODS RECEIVED FROM SUPPLIERS ON CREDIT

Goods received documentation is signed in by the goods-in manager, M Gillibert, who also checks the unit prices against the purchase orders. You then have to check suppliers' terms and conditions and the calculations on suppliers' invoices before passing them for payment (which is normally made when the statement is received).

You also check suppliers' credit notes when they are received to make sure that the correct discount and VAT has been applied.

PETTY CASH

The petty cash is controlled in the normal day-to-day running of the business by Jessie Page. Your job is to check the vouchers and receipts and to write up the petty cash book on a regular basis.

PAYROLL

Jessie Page has six employees on the payroll which is run on a weekly basis. This will not, of course, include her own drawings from the business as sole owner. The payroll is operated on a manual basis. You complete the deductions sheets, a payroll analysis sheet and the payslips each week. Employees are paid through the Albion Bank 'Auto Credit' BACS payment system – you have to complete a bank schedule with the employee payment details. The total of the net pay is automatically deducted from the bank account when the sheet is received by the bank.

Details of income tax and net National Insurance Contributions to the Inland Revenue are entered weekly on a PAYE summary sheet. The monthly totals from this sheet are sent each month on a bank giro payment (P30B) to the Inland Revenue.

ACCOUNTING RECORDS

Frontpage Stationery records purchases invoices in a purchases day book, and credit notes received in a purchases returns day book. A manual system of double-entry book-keeping is used, with a cash book and a main (general) ledger. The main ledger includes a control account for creditors, with supplier accounts contained in a subsidiary (purchases) ledger.

TASKS

PART 1: DEALING WITH CREDIT PURCHASES

1 Refer to the suppliers' invoices and related goods received notes on pages 166 to 171. The goods received notes have already been checked against the purchase orders. You are required to perform your usual validation checks on the invoices and to set out your results on the form provided on page 172. You should indicate either that the invoice is approved for payment, or that it is not approved. If it is not approved, you should state clearly the reason(s) why you are not approving it, and the follow-up action you would take. You usually raise invoice queries by letter.

Today's date is 25 July 2001.

2 If there are any invoices which you have not approved, you are required to write an appropriate letter to the supplier(s). The letters (page 173 - 174) should set out the problem and ask for the appropriate action to be taken.

Use your own name and the date 25 July 2001.

3 Refer to the purchases day book on page 194 which has already been written up to 24 July 2001.

You are to enter all the purchases invoices which you have approved in task 1 into the purchases day book.

Total the purchases day book and record the accounting entries in the main (general) ledger and subsidiary (purchases) ledger accounts on pages 194 to 198.

Note: opening balances are shown on these accounts where appropriate.

4 On 27 July 2001 you receive a credit note from Meara Limited, one of your regular suppliers (page 175). The credit was agreed earlier in the month and so does not apply to invoice 423 (Task 1, page 169). You are to check the credit note for arithmetic accuracy and for the trade discount applied.

If there is any problem you are to send an e-mail. Draft the text on the e-mail on page 175. Draft the e-mail for the attention of the Accounts Department and sign off with your own name.

5 Refer to the purchases returns day book on page 194 which has already been written up to 24 July 2001.

Total the purchases returns day book and record the accounting entries in the main (general) ledger and subsidiary (purchases) ledger accounts on pages 194 to 198.

PART 2: MAKING AND RECORDING PAYMENTSS

6 On 31 July 2001 Jessie passes you four invoices received in June which have been approved and are now due for payment (pages 176 to 177). She also passes you two approved invoices which qualify for cash discount (page178).

You are to complete the remittance advices and cheques in payment of the six invoices (pages 179 to 184). The remittance advices and cheques should be dated 31 July 2001 but the cheques left unsigned – Jessie Page will sign them when she has checked them.

7 On 27 July 2001 you process the payroll for the six employees of Frontpage Stationery. You have completed a payroll analysis sheet (page 185) from the deduction sheets.

You are to complete an Albion Bank 'Auto Credit' BACS payment schedule (page 186) with the employee payment details from the employment record sheet (page 187) ready for signature by Jessie Page.

The total of the net pay is automatically deducted from the bank account when the sheet is received by the bank.

8 Transfer the information from the payroll analysis sheet into the main (general) ledger accounts for wages & salaries, Inland Revenue, pension fund, and wages & salaries control – these accounts are on pages 196 and 197. Date the entries 27 July 2001.

Note: opening balances are shown on these accounts where appropriate.

9 Record in the cash book (page 196) the six payment cheques from task 6 and the total of the payroll BACS payment schedule from task 7.

10 Total the cash book and make the entries in the main (general) ledger and subsidiary (purchases) ledger accounts on pages 194 to 198.

11 On 3 August 2001 you are to complete the PAYE deduction summary (page 187). The deduction figures for the first two weeks are already there. You extract the figures for the third week from the payroll analysis sheet (page 185). The figures for the fourth week are:

Income tax collected	£225.00
National Insurance Contributions (employee)	£128.00
National Insurance Contributions (employer)	£156.00

12 Complete the P30B and cheque (page 188) with the PAYE amounts from the PAYE deduction summary (page 187). The cheque is to be made payable to the Inland Revenue and should be dated 3 August 2001; it will be signed by Jessie Page. The P30B will be paid in by yourself on 6 August 2001.

13 Jessie Page operates a petty cash system. The imprest amount is £200.

The guide shown at the top of the next page is written on a sheet of paper which is kept in the petty cash drawer in Jessie's office.

FRONTPAGE PETTY CASH

APPROVED EXPENSES THAT CAN BE REIMBURSED
(Maximum amount claimable £50)
Petrol or diesel fuel (this can only be claimed by sales representatives)
Stationery
Window cleaning (to be analysed as office expenses)
Travelling expenses (only for business purposes)
Stamps and postage
Tea, coffee etc (to be analysed as office expenses).

EXPENSES ON WHICH VAT IS PAYABLE (provided the supplier is VAT registered)
Petrol or diesel fuel
Stationery
Window cleaning
Taxi fares

The date is 3 August 2001 and you have been asked to update the petty cash system. Jessie has topped up the cash box on 1 August to restore the balance to the imprest amount of £200. This opening balance of £200 is shown in the petty cash book (page 189).

You have been presented with ten claims on petty cash vouchers. These are shown, along with supporting receipts where available, on pages 190 to 193.

You are required to authorise those claims which you think are valid and which can be reimbursed out of petty cash. You must sign in your own name in the 'authorised' section of the the appropriate petty cash vouchers.

If you are rejecting any claims you should write the reason on the voucher.

14 All the vouchers which you have authorised are to be entered in the Petty Cash Book provided on page 189. You will have to work out the VAT content of any of the payments which involve VAT (the supplier must be registered for VAT if you are doing this).

The analysis columns must be completed as appropriate.

Total the columns, but do not balance the petty cash book.

INVOICE
FURLONG LIMITED
37 Highfield Trading Estate Lampeter LL4 7YG

invoice to

Frontpage Stationery
Unit 2, Hillside Trading Estate
Knightwick
MR6 7LP

invoice no 7724

account 246

your reference 377

date/tax point 20 07 01

product code	description	quantity	price	unit	total	discount 0%	net
844	Calculator SRP22	30	6.10	each	183.00	0.00	183.00
2634	Dictaphone Z11	25	42.00	each	1050.00	0.00	1050.00

goods total	1233.00
VAT	215.77
TOTAL	1448.77

terms
Net 30 days

INVOICE
Sheppard & Suckling
Hanover House, Lilly Square, London SW3 6BZ

invoice to

Frontpage Stationery
Unit 2, Hillside Trading Estate
Knightwick
MR6 7LP

invoice no 2705

account 4226

your reference 390

date/tax point 18 07 01

product code	description	quantity	price	unit	total	discount 5%	net
B34	Laminated UK map	8	8.80	each	70.40	3.52	66.88
R219	A2 Desk planner	12	9.60	each	115.20	5.76	109.44

goods total	176.32
VAT	30.85
TOTAL	207.17

terms
Net 30 days

INVOICE

Drysdale & Co

13 Berkeley Street, London E4 3BZ

invoice to

Frontpage Stationery
Unit 2, Hillside Trading Estate
Knightwick
MR6 7LP

invoice no 2721

account 5291

your reference 385

date/tax point 20 07 01

product code	description	quantity	price	unit	total	discount 2%	net
5R80	White copy paper 80g	30	5.60	box	280.00	5.60	274.40
MEC5	Manila envelopes C5	50	7.30	box	365.00	7.30	357.70

goods total	632.10
VAT	108.95
TOTAL	741.05

terms
1.5% cash discount 14 day settlement,
Net 30 days

INVOICE

Drysdale & Co

13 Berkeley Street, London E4 3BZ

invoice to

Frontpage Stationery
Unit 2, Hillside Trading Estate
Knightwick
MR6 7LP

invoice no 2849

account 5291

your reference 402

date/tax point 23 07 01

product code	description	quantity	price	unit	total	discount 2%	net
T4000	Tabulabels, 4000 box	40	14.25	box	570.00	11.40	558.60
FX98	Calculator FX98	30	4.80	each	144.00	2.88	141.12

goods total	699.72
VAT	120.61
TOTAL	820.33

terms
1.5% cash discount 14 day settlement,
Net 30 days

INVOICE
Soloman Limited
Bevels Drive, Hornsea, N11 5TG

invoice to

Frontpage Stationery
Unit 2, Hillside Trading Estate
Knightwick
MR6 7LP

invoice no 149
account 435
your reference 381
date/tax point 18 07 01

product code	description	quantity	price	unit	total	discount 0%	net
180	Photocopier FP180	2	485.00	each	970.00	0.00	970.00

goods total	970.00
VAT	169.75
TOTAL	1139.75

terms
Net 30 days

INVOICE
Nogan Limited
316 Pearse Road, Jackleton AD3 4PY

invoice to

Frontpage Stationery
Unit 2, Hillside Trading Estate
Knightwick
MR6 7LP

invoice no 516
account 3241
your reference 385
date/tax point 20 07 01

product code	description	quantity	price	unit	total	discount 0%	net
244	Flexi desk light	4	23.00	each	92.00	0.00	92.00
234	Floor uplighter	6	18.50	each	111.00	0.00	111.00
441	Bubble jet printer	1	175.00	each	175.00	0.00	175.00

goods total	378.00
VAT	66.15
TOTAL	444.15

terms
Net 30 days

INVOICE

Putney Limited
Unit 17 Bancroft Estate
Droysley MD14 6ZX

invoice to

Frontpage Stationery
Unit 2, Hillside Trading Estate
Knightwick
MR6 7LP

invoice no 3492

account 4216

your reference 388

date/tax point 17 07 01

product code	description	quantity	price	unit	total	discount 3%	net
67B	Box files	120	2.10	each	252.00	7.56	244.44
442	Portable fan	6	18.00	each	108.00	3.24	104.76

goods total	349.20
VAT	61.11
TOTAL	410.31

terms
Net 30 days

INVOICE

Meara Limited
45 Crystal Dock,
Thimborough BD17 2ER

invoice to

Frontpage Stationery
Unit 2, Hillside Trading Estate
Knightwick
MR6 7LP

invoice no 423

account 2711

your reference 392

date/tax point 20 07 01

product code	description	quantity	price	unit	total	discount 5%	net
LP34	Laser printer	2	380.00	each	760.00	38.00	722.00

goods total	722.00
VAT	126.35
TOTAL	848.35

terms
Net 30 days

GOODS RECEIVED NOTE no 2143

Date	*23 July 2001*
Supplier	*Drysdale & Co*
Order no.	*364*

quantity	description
30 boxes	*White copy paper 80g*
50 boxes	*Manila envelopes C5*

received in good condition

M Gillibert

GOODS RECEIVED NOTE no 2144

Date	*23 July 2001*
Supplier	*Soloman Ltd*
Order no.	*381*

quantity	description
2	*Photocopier FP180*

received in good condition

M Gillibert

GOODS RECEIVED NOTE no 2145

Date	*23 July 2001*
Supplier	*Nogan Ltd*
Order no.	*385*

quantity	description
4	*Flexi desk light*
6	*Floor uplighter*

received in good condition

M Gillibert

GOODS RECEIVED NOTE no 2146

Date	*23 July 2001*
Supplier	*Furlong Ltd*
Order no.	*377*

quantity	description
30	*Calculator SRP22*
25	*Dictaphone Z11*

received in good condition

M Gillibert

GOODS RECEIVED NOTE no 2147

Date *23 July 2001*
Supplier *Putney Ltd*
Order no. *388*

quantity	description
120	*Box files*
6	*Portable fans*

received in good condition

M Gillibert

GOODS RECEIVED NOTE no 2148

Date *23 July 2001*
Supplier *Meara Ltd*
Order no. *392*

quantity	description
2	*Laser Printer*

received in good condition

M Gillibert

GOODS RECEIVED NOTE no 2149

Date *23 July 2001*
Supplier *Sheppard & Suckling*
Order no. *390*

quantity	description
8	*Laminated UK map*
12	*A2 Desk planner*

received in good condition

M Gillibert

GOODS RECEIVED NOTE no 2150

Date *23 July 2001*
Supplier *Drysdale & Co*
Order no. *402*

quantity	description
40 boxes	*Tabulabels*
30	*Calculator FX98*

received in good condition

M Gillibert

Supplier/invoice	Action

FRONTPAGE STATIONERY

Unit 2 Hillside Trading Estate, Knightwick, MR6 7LP

Tel 01923 230399 Fax 01923 237995 E-mail frontpage@goblin.com

www.frontpage.co.uk

VAT Reg 2342 6171 89

FRONTPAGE STATIONERY

Unit 2 Hillside Trading Estate, Knightwick, MR6 7LP

Tel 01923 230399 Fax 01923 237995 E-mail frontpage@goblin.com

www.frontpage.co.uk

VAT Reg 2342 6171 89

CREDIT NOTE

Meara Limited

45 Crystal Dock,
Thimborough BD17 2ER

invoice to

Frontpage Stationery
Unit 2, Hillside Trading Estate
Knightwick
MR6 7LP

credit note no	423
account	2711
your reference	301
date/tax point	25 07 01

product code	description	quantity	price	unit	total	discount	net
SC03	Imax21 colour scanner	1	400.00	each	400.00	00.00	400.00

goods total	400.00
VAT	17.50
TOTAL	417.50

reason for credit
Cancelled order – credit as agreed.

To address <mearaltd@netserve.com>
From:<frontpage@goblin.com>

Subject:

Date:

INVOICE
FURLONG LIMITED
37 Highfield Trading Estate Lampeter LL4 7YG

invoice to

Frontpage Stationery
Unit 2, Hillside Trading Estate
Knightwick
MR6 7LP

invoice no	7714
account	246
your reference	333
date/tax point	20 06 01

product code	description	quantity	price	unit	total	discount 0%	net
107BK	Box files (black)	10	5.45	each	54.50	0.00	54.50

terms
Net 30 days

goods total	54.50
VAT	9.53
TOTAL	64.03

INVOICE
Sheppard & Suckling
Hanover House, Lilly Square, London SW3 6BZ

invoice to

Frontpage Stationery
Unit 2, Hillside Trading Estate
Knightwick
MR6 7LP

invoice no	2680
account	4226
your reference	301
date/tax point	13 06 01

product code	description	quantity	price	unit	total	discount 5%	net
4531	Photocopy paper white	18	4.90	ream	88.20	4.41	83.79

terms
Net 30 days

goods total	83.79
VAT	14.66
TOTAL	98.45

INVOICE

Soloman Limited

Bevels Drive, Hornsea, N11 5TG

invoice to

Frontpage Stationery
Unit 2, Hillside Trading Estate
Knightwick
MR6 7LP

invoice no 120

account 435

your reference 335

date/tax point 18 06 01

product code	description	quantity	price	unit	total	discount 0%	net
74523	Hermes fax machine	1	285.00	each	285.00	0.00	285.00

goods total	285.00
VAT	49.87
TOTAL	334.87

terms
Net 30 days

INVOICE

Putney Limited

Unit 17 Bancroft Estate
Droysley MD14 6ZX

invoice to

Frontpage Stationery
Unit 2, Hillside Trading Estate
Knightwick
MR6 7LP

invoice no 3411

account 4216

your reference 271

date/tax point 15 06 01

product code	description	quantity	price	unit	total	discount 3%	net
442	Portable fan	2	18.00	each	36.00	1.08	34.92

goods total	34.92
VAT	6.11
TOTAL	41.03

terms
Net 30 days

INVOICE

Drysdale & Co

13 Berkeley Street, London E4 3BZ

invoice to

Frontpage Stationery
Unit 2, Hillside Trading Estate
Knightwick
MR6 7LP

invoice no 2657

account 5291

your reference 364

date/tax point 18 07 01

product code	description	quantity	price	unit	total	discount 2%	net
6546	Operator chair	2	78.00	each	156.00	3.12	152.88

goods total	152.88
VAT	26.35
TOTAL	179.23

terms
1.5% cash discount 14 day settlement,
Net 30 days

INVOICE

Drysdale & Co

13 Berkeley Street, London E4 3BZ

invoice to

Frontpage Stationery
Unit 2, Hillside Trading Estate
Knightwick
MR6 7LP

invoice no 2684

account 5291

your reference 367

date/tax point 19 07 01

product code	description	quantity	price	unit	total	discount 2%	net
3534	Apex laminator	1	199.50	each	199.50	3.99	195.51

goods total	195.51
VAT	33.70
TOTAL	229.21

terms
1.5% cash discount 14 day settlement,
Net 30 days

TO

REMITTANCE ADVICE

FROM

Frontpage Stationery
Unit 2, Hillside Trading Estate
Knightwick
MR6 7LP

Account

Date

date	your reference	our reference	payment amount

CHEQUE TOTAL £

Albion Bank PLC
7 High Street
Mereford BR1 2AJ

Date

90 43 15

Pay

A/c payee only

£

FRONTPAGE STATIONERY

083800 90 43 15 17256741

TO

REMITTANCE ADVICE

FROM

Frontpage Stationery
Unit 2, Hillside Trading Estate
Knightwick
MR6 7LP

Account

Date

date	your reference	our reference	payment amount

CHEQUE TOTAL £

Albion Bank PLC
7 High Street
Mereford BR1 2AJ

Date

90 43 15

Pay

A/c payee only

£

FRONTPAGE STATIONERY

083801 90 43 15 17256741

TO

REMITTANCE ADVICE

FROM

Frontpage Stationery
Unit 2, Hillside Trading Estate
Knightwick
MR6 7LP

Account

Date

date	your reference	our reference	payment amount

CHEQUE TOTAL £

Albion Bank PLC
7 High Street
Mereford BR1 2AJ

Date

90 43 15

Pay

A/c payee only

£

FRONTPAGE STATIONERY

083802 90 43 15 17256741

TO

REMITTANCE ADVICE

FROM

Frontpage Stationery
Unit 2, Hillside Trading Estate
Knightwick
MR6 7LP

Account

Date

date	your reference	our reference	payment amount

CHEQUE TOTAL £

Albion Bank PLC
7 High Street
Mereford BR1 2AJ

Date

90 43 15

Pay

A/c payee only

£

FRONTPAGE STATIONERY

083803 90 43 15 17256741

TO

REMITTANCE ADVICE

FROM

Frontpage Stationery
Unit 2, Hillside Trading Estate
Knightwick
MR6 7LP

Account

Date

date	your reference	our reference	payment amount

CHEQUE TOTAL £

Albion Bank PLC
7 High Street
Mereford BR1 2AJ

Date

90 43 15

Pay

A/c payee only

£

FRONTPAGE STATIONERY

083804 90 43 15 17256741

TO

REMITTANCE ADVICE

FROM

Frontpage Stationery
Unit 2, Hillside Trading Estate
Knightwick
MR6 7LP

Account

Date

date	your reference	our reference	payment amount

CHEQUE TOTAL £

Albion Bank PLC
7 High Street
Mereford BR1 2AJ

Date

90 43 15

Pay

A/c payee only

£

FRONTPAGE STATIONERY

083805 90 43 15 17256741

FRONTPAGE STATIONERY **payroll analysis sheet** **Week ending** 27 July 2001

employee reference	employee name	Earnings				Deductions				Employer's National Insurance Contributions	Employer's Pension Contributions	Net Pay
		Basic £	Overtime £	Bonus £	Total Gross Pay £	Income Tax £	National Insurance £	Pension Contributions £	Total Deductions £	£	£	£
2345	B Shaw	205.00	25.00	15.00	245.00	35.00	19.50	10.25	64.75	24.50	10.25	180.25
2346	S O'Casey	205.00	10.00	15.00	230.00	32.50	18.00	10.25	60.75	23.05	10.25	169.25
2347	J Osborne	205.00	25.00	15.00	245.00	35.00	19.50	-	54.50	24.50	-	190.50
2348	H Winter	205.00	25.00	15.00	245.00	35.00	19.50	-	54.50	24.50	-	190.50
2349	L Klein	205.00	10.00	15.00	230.00	32.50	18.00	10.25	60.75	23.05	10.25	169.25
2350	T Manning	205.00	25.00	15.00	245.00	35.00	19.50	10.25	64.75	24.50	10.25	180.25
TOTALS		1230.00	120.00	90.00	1440.00	205.00	114.00	41.00	360.00	144.10	41.00	1080.00

Albion Bank PLC
Auto Credit System

Bank branch....Mereford....

Originator name..Frontpage Stationery.....reference...356345....

Date...27-07-01....

Bank sort code	*Account no*	*Name*	*Payee no*	*Amount*
			PAYMENT TOTAL	

Please make the above payments to reach the payees on ....31 07 01....(date)

Please debit account no..........with the sum of £..........

authorised signature..........

EMPLOYEE DATABASE

Employee	bank sort code	account number	payee number
B Shaw	45-45-62	10386394	1246
S O'Casey	56-67-23	22347342	1250
J Osborne	40-47-07	42472411	1267
H Winter	76-87-44	56944491	1271
L Klein	33-00-77	23442413	1272
T Manning	59-99-01	46244703	1273

PAYE DEDUCTION SUMMARY

week ending	income tax £	NICs (employee) £	NICs (employer) £
13 July 2001	*195.00*	*95.00*	*115.00*
20 July 2001	*201.00*	*105.00*	*135.00*
27 July 2001			
3 August 2001			
TOTALS	**income tax**		
	NICs (employee)		
	NICs (employer)		
	TOTAL PAYE TO P30B		

Albion Bank PLC
7 High Street
Mereford BR1 2AJ

Date

90 43 15

Pay

A/c payee only

£

FRONTPAGE STATIONERY

083812 90 43 15 17256741

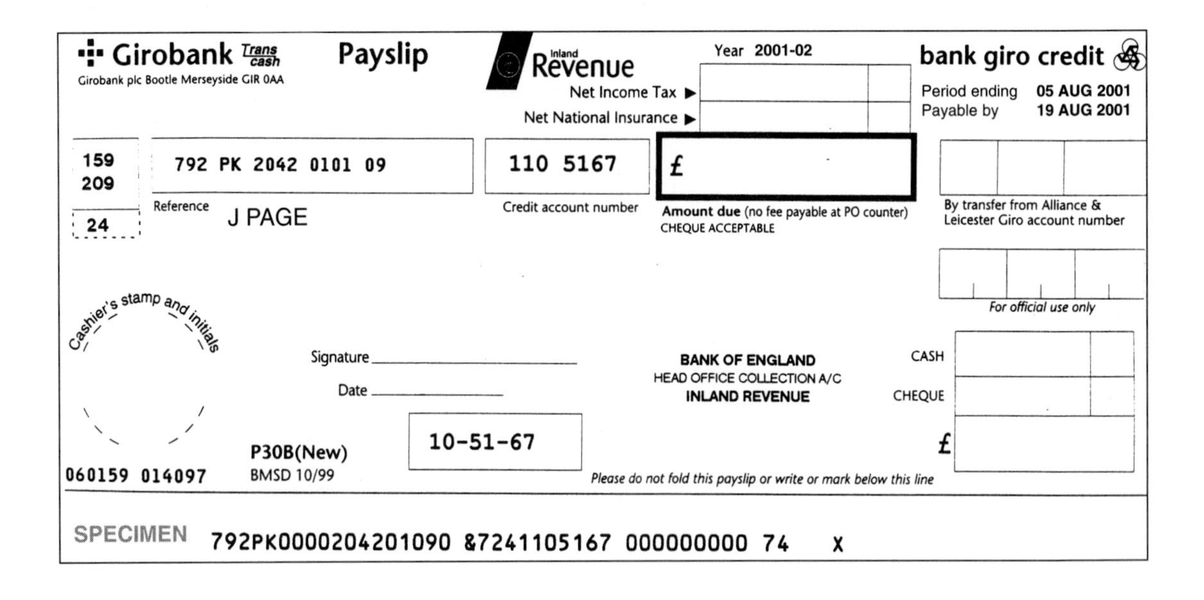

Girobank Trans cash
Girobank plc Bootle Merseyside GIR 0AA

Payslip

Inland Revenue

Year 2001-02

Net Income Tax ▶

Net National Insurance ▶

bank giro credit

Period ending **05 AUG 2001**
Payable by **19 AUG 2001**

159
209
24

792 PK 2042 0101 09

Reference J PAGE

110 5167

Credit account number

£

Amount due (no fee payable at PO counter)
CHEQUE ACCEPTABLE

By transfer from Alliance & Leicester Giro account number

For official use only

Cashier's stamp and initials

Signature

Date

BANK OF ENGLAND
HEAD OFFICE COLLECTION A/C
INLAND REVENUE

CASH

CHEQUE

£

10-51-67

P30B(New)
BMSD 10/99

060159 014097

Please do not fold this payslip or write or mark below this line

SPECIMEN 792PK0000204201090 &7241105167 000000000 74 X

PETTY CASH BOOK

Receipts	Date	Details	Voucher No.	Payment	Analysis columns					
					VAT	Postage	Stationery	Office Expenses	Petrol/ diesel	Travel Expenses
£ 200.00	2001 1 Aug	Balance b/f		£	£	£	£	£	£	£

PETTY CASH VOUCHER No *800*

Date *1 August 2001*

	£	p
Computer disks	*107*	*86*
	107	*86*

Signature *B Shaw* Authorised

PETTY CASH VOUCHER No *801*

Date *1 August 2001*

	£	p
Stamps	*9*	*50*
	9	*50*

Signature *B Shaw* Authorised

PETTY CASH VOUCHER No *802*

Date *2 August 2001*

	£	p
Petrol	*20*	*00*
	20	*00*

Signature *H Winter* Authorised

PETTY CASH VOUCHER No *803*

Date *2 August 2001*

	£	p
Taxi fare	*3*	*85*
	3	*85*

Signature *H Winter* Authorised

PETTY CASH VOUCHER No *804*

Date *3 August 2001*

	£	p
Postage on parcel	*6*	*20*
	6	*20*

Signature *T Manning* Authorised

PETTY CASH VOUCHER No *805*

Date *1 August 2001*

	£	p
Tea and coffee	*5*	*60*
	5	*60*

Signature *L Klein* Authorised

PETTY CASH VOUCHER No *806*

Date *1 August 2001*

	£	p
Petrol	*28*	*00*
	28	*00*

Signature *T Manning* Authorised

PETTY CASH VOUCHER No *807*

Date *2 August 2001*

	£	p
Envelopes	*11*	*25*
	11	*25*

Signature *L Klein* Authorised

PETTY CASH VOUCHER No *808*

Date *1 August 2001*

	£	p
Window cleaning	*8*	*00*
	8	*00*

Signature *B Shaw* Authorised

PETTY CASH VOUCHER No *809*

Date *2 August 2001*

	£	p
Taxi fare	*11*	*28*
	11	*28*

Signature *J Osborne* Authorised

supporting documents . . .

INVOICE

COMPUTER SUPPLIES LIMITED

16 HARLEY WAY MANCHESTER M3 6BY
Tel 0161 429 5314 Fax 0161 429 5951 Email toni@cool.u-net.com
VAT Reg GB 0745 4672 71

invoice to

Frontpage Stationery
Unit 2, Hillside Trading Estate
Knightwick
MR6 7LP

invoice no	2714
account	3993
your reference	47609
date/tax point	01 08 01

product code	description	quantity	price	unit	total	discount %	net
244	Zipo computer disks HD, PC formatted	18	5.10	box	91.80	0.00	91.80

goods total	91.80
VAT	16.06
TOTAL	107.86

terms
Payable on delivery

POST OFFICE	Receipt
Stamps	*£9.50*
TOTAL	*£9.50*

HYLTON FUEL
Hylton Road, Worcester WR2 5GN
VAT Reg 101 7543 26

22 litres unleaded	20.00
Cash tendered	20.00

02.08.01 14.23

purchase by a sales representative

Maxi Minicabs
Enstone Road, Martley, MR2 4JL

RECEIVED £ *3.85*

VAT Reg 229 7543 26

taxi to work when car would not start

POST OFFICE	**Receipt**
Parcel postage	*£6.20*
TOTAL	*£6.20*

VALUE FOODSTORE
23 JOHN STREET WYTHENFORD

Tea	2.70
Coffee	2.90
Total	5.60
Cash tendered	10.00
Change	4.40

01.08.01 10.30

Star Stationery
Deansgate, Mereford MR1 3RT
VAT Reg 333 7804 01

02.08.01 09.30

200 envelopes C4	11.25
Total	11.25
Cash tendered	12.00
Change	00.75

Phil Johns, Windowcleaning
23 Garden Road, Sapley, MR9 4GF

RECEIVED £ *8.00*

Phil Johns is not registered for VAT

Maxi Minicabs
Enstone Road, Martley, MR2 4JL

RECEIVED £ *11.28*

VAT Reg 229 7543 26

taxi to railway station for business trip

PURCHASES DAY BOOK

Date 2001	*Details*	*Invoice No*	*Total* £ p	*VAT* £ p	*Net* £ p
23 Jul	Sheppard & Suckling	2654	481.56	71.72	409.84
23 Jul	Drysdale & Co	2657	179.23	26.35	152.88
23 Jul	Nogan Limited	489	455.37	67.82	387.55
24 Jul	Meara Limited	407	1,438.91	214.30	1,224.61
24 Jul	Drysdale & Co	2684	229.21	33.70	195.51
24 Jul	Furlong Limited	7671	1,009.32	150.32	859.00
24 Jul	Putney Limited	3434	699.87	104.23	595.64

PURCHASES RETURNS DAY BOOK

Date 2001	*Details*	*Credit Note No*	*Total* £ p	*VAT* £ p	*Net* £ p
23 Jul	Soloman Limited	854	115.62	17.22	98.40
23 Jul	Meara Limited	415	78.30	11.66	66.64
24 Jul	Nogan Limited	103	104.45	15.55	88.90

MAIN (GENERAL) LEDGER

Purchases

Date 2001	*Details*	*Amount* £ p	*Date* 2001	*Details*	*Amount* £ p
23 Jul	Balance b/d	194,246.55			

Purchases returns

Date 2001	Details	Amount £ p	Date 2001	Details	Amount £ p
			23 Jul	Balance b/d	6,274.83

Creditors control

Date 2001	Details	Amount £ p	Date 2001	Details	Amount £ p
			23 Jul	Balance b/d	35,201.26

Value Added Tax

Date 2001	Details	Amount £ p	Date 2001	Details	Amount £ p
			23 Jul	Balance b/d	8,321.35

Discount received

Date 2001	Details	Amount £ p	Date 2001	Details	Amount £ p
			23 Jul	Balance b/d	354.61

Cash Book: Payments

Date 2001	Details	Discount received £ p	Cash £ p	Bank £ p

MAIN (GENERAL) LEDGER (continued)

Wages & salaries

Date 2001	Details	Amount £ p	Date 2001	Details	Amount £ p
23 Jul	Balance b/d	24,784.30			

Inland Revenue

Date 2001	Details	Amount £ p	Date 2001	Details	Amount £ p
			23 Jul	Balance b/d	846.00

Pension fund

Date 2001	Details	Amount £ p	Date 2001	Details	Amount £ p
			23 Jul	Balance b/d	164.00

Wages & salaries control

Date 2001	Details	Amount £ p	Date 2001	Details	Amount £ p

SUBSIDIARY (PURCHASES) LEDGER

Drysdale & Co

Date 2001	Details	Amount £ p	Date 2001	Details	Amount £ p

Furlong Limited

Date 2001	Details	Amount £ p	Date 2001	Details	Amount £ p
			23 Jul	Balance b/d	954.28

Meara Limited

Date 2001	Details	Amount £ p	Date 2001	Details	Amount £ p
			23 Jul	Balance b/d	3,390.86

Nogan Limited

Date 2001	Details	Amount £ p	Date 2001	Details	Amount £ p
			23 Jul	Balance b/d	1,974.26

Putney Limited

Date 2001	Details	Amount £ p	Date 2001	Details	Amount £ p
			23 Jul	Balance b/d	807.54

Sheppard & Suckling

Date 2001	Details	Amount £ p	Date 2001	Details	Amount £ p
			23 Jul	Balance b/d	98.45

Soloman Limited

Date 2001	Details	Amount £ p	Date 2001	Details	Amount £ p
			23 Jul	Balance b/d	756.81

Unit 3 Practice Simulation

Sunny Days Garden Supplies

suggested time 3 hours

SCENARIO

This Simulation is based on 'Sunny Days', a business which buys garden furniture and equipment from manufacturers and sells to garden centres and specialist shops. The tasks in the Simulation include:

- preparation of trial balances
- entering balances from the trial balance into accounts in the main (general) ledger
- restoring the imprest amount of petty cash book and balancing the account
- checking the bank statement against the cash book for accuracy, and updating the cash book as necessary
- the operation of debtor and creditor control accounts, and agreeing the balances with the subsidiary ledgers
- journal entries
- the use of a stock record card

NVQ UNIT 3 – ELEMENTS COVERED

1. balance bank transactions
2. prepare ledger balances and control accounts
3. draft an initial trial balance

PRACTICE SIMULATION SUNNY DAYS GARDEN SUPPLIES

unit 3

SITUATION

'Sunny Days' is a business which buys garden furniture and equipment from manufacturers and sells to garden centres and specialist shops. The business is registered for Value Added Tax.

The book-keeping is operated on a manual system, but the payroll is calculated using a computer program. The main (general) ledger includes control accounts for debtors and creditors (with customer and supplier accounts contained in subsidiary ledgers), cash control account for petty cash (with petty cash book forming the subsidiary ledger), and wages control account (with details taken from the payroll analysis).

You have just started work as an accounts clerk and are responsible for all aspects of the book-keeping system, including payroll. Your supervisor is Jane Jagpal, the office manager. A part-time accounts assistant, Mike Venn, helps you with the book-keeping.

TASKS

Today is 31 July 2001 and you only started working for 'Sunny Days' last week. There are a number of tasks that need to be completed today.

1 A trial balance was not prepared at the end of last month, on 30 June 2001. A list of the balances of all the accounts at that date is given below. Transfer the balances to the relevant columns of the trial balance shown on page 206. Total each column: the debit column and credit column totals should be the same.

Balances at 30 June 2001

	£
Purchases	227,435
Sales	362,024
Purchases returns	3,217
Sales returns	10,309
Discount allowed	1,482
Discount received	793
Wages	88,463
Rent paid	5,721
Rates	3,084
Bank charges	396
Postages	2,787
Stationery	1,824
Travel	2,796

Bad debts written off	427
Sundry expenses	3,048
Vehicles	12,000
Office equipment	6,000
Stock	38,435
Cash control	100
Bank (debit balance)	14,976
Debtors control	102,371
Creditors control	75,284
Value Added Tax (credit balance)	3,335
Inland Revenue (credit balance)	3,076
Bank loan	15,000
Capital	75,000
Drawings	16,075

2 Enter the balances from the trial balance (Task 1) into the following accounts shown on pages 207 to 211:

Purchases
Sales
Purchases returns
Sales returns
Discount allowed
Discount received
Wages
Rent paid
Rates
Bank charges
Postages
Stationery
Travel
Bad debts written off
Sundry expenses
Cash control
Debtors control
Creditors control
Value Added Tax
Inland Revenue

Notes:

- *enter the balances as 'balance b/d' using the date 1 July 2001*
- *other accounts from the trial balance, which are not listed above, are not required to be opened*

3 The petty cash book for July has been written up by your assistant, Mike Venn, and is shown on page 212.

Total the columns and restore the imprest amount to £100 on 31 July 2001 – cash is to be withdrawn from the bank account using cheque number 101281, and the appropriate entry made in the cash book on page 213. Balance the petty cash book.

Complete the double-entry transactions from petty cash book using the accounts shown on pages 207 to 211.

4 The cash book for July 2001 has been written up during the month by your assistant, Mike Venn.

- Update the cash book on page 213 from the schedules of standing orders, direct debits and bank giro credits shown on page 212.
- Check the bank statement on page 213 against the cash book for accuracy, and update the cash book as necessary.
- Total the cash book, showing clearly the balance carried down.
- List the reasons why the balance in the cash book does not agree with the balance on the bank statement (use page 214 for your answer).
- Complete double-entry from the cash book to the main (general) ledger for the following accounts (shown on pages 207 to 211).

  Inland Revenue

  Rent paid

  Rates

  Bank charges

  Debtors control (see list of debtors below)

  Creditors control (see list of creditors below)

To assist with this task, Mike Venn provides you with a list of the debtors and creditors of Sunny Days:

debtors	**creditors**
C & R Garden Centres	Alpha Manufacturing
Garden Time Limited	Dayton and Company
Osborne plc	Eveshore Woodwork
Raven Enterprises	RP Industries
Tyax Country Stores	Tritton Limited
Western DIY	Wyvern Wood

Notes:

- *where appropriate, Mike Venn will make the entries in the subsidiary ledgers*
- *the payment for wages will be recorded in wages control account in a later task (task 8)*

5 Your assistant, Mike Venn, has kept the subsidiary (purchases) ledger up-to-date during the month. He provides you with the list of balances at 31 July 2001 shown on page 214. The totals of the purchases day book and purchases returns day book, and the total of discount received for the month are also shown on page 214.

- Record the double-entry from the day books and the discount total in the main (general) ledger for the following accounts (shown on pages 207 to 211):

  Purchases

  Purchases returns

  Discount received

  Creditors control

  Value Added Tax

- Total the creditors control account at 31 July 2001, showing clearly the balance carried down (do not balance any other accounts at this stage).
- Reconcile the balance of the creditors control account with the list of balances for the subsidiary (purchases) ledger. Use page 214 for your answer.

6 The office manager, Jane Jagpal, passes you two journal entries (below) which she has approved.

Record the journal entries in the double-entry accounts in the main (general) ledger. (Note: Mike Venn will make any relevant entries in the subsidiary ledgers.)

JOURNAL

Date	Details	Debit	Credit
2001		£	£
31 Jul	Bad debts written off account	440	
	VAT account	77	
	Debtors control account		517
		517	517
	Amount owed by Woodland Garden Centre written off as a bad debt		
	Approved: Jane Jagpal		
	Date: 31 Jul 2001		
31 Jul	Travel account	50	
	Sundry expenses account		50
	Correction of error: fuel for vehicles posted in error to sundry expenses account		
	Approved: Jane Jagpal		
	Date: 31 Jul 2001		

7 Your assistant, Mike Venn, has kept the subsidiary (sales) ledger up-to-date during the month. He provides you with the list of balances at 31 July 2001 shown on page 215. The totals of the sales day book and sales returns day book, and the total of discount allowed for the month are also shown on page 215.

- Record the double-entry from the day books and the discount total in the main (general) ledger for the following accounts (shown on pages 207 to 211):

  Sales

  Sales returns

  Discount allowed

  Debtors control

  Value Added Tax

- Total the debtors control account at 31 July 2001, showing clearly the balance carried down (do not balance any other accounts at this stage).
- Reconcile the balance of the debtors control account with the list of balances from the subsidiary (sales) ledger. If there is an imbalance, make a note to Jane Jagpal, office manager, suggesting where the error may be. Use pages 215 and 216 for your answer.

8 The computer printout for wages for July 2001 is summarised on page 216.

- Complete the wages and salaries control account (page 216) with the figures from the July payroll. Total the account.
- Complete the double-entry transactions from wages and salaries control account into the main (general) ledger accounts shown on pages 207 to 211 (note: the bank payment for net pay is already recorded in bank account).

9 Sunny Days buys in plastic garden chairs of the 'Relaxa' brand from RP Industries. Today, a physical stock take of the chairs showed there were 360 in stock at a cost of £20 each, giving a stock valuation of £7,200.

Jane Jagpal gives you the stock record card shown on page 217 and asks you to complete it and to make a reconciliation with the physical stock take. If there is an imbalance, make a note to Jane suggesting where the error may be. Use page 218 for your answer.

10
- Balance all the main (general) ledger accounts shown on pages 207 to 211 at 31 July 2001, showing clearly the balance carried down.
- Transfer the balances to the trial balance on page 219.
- Transfer the balance of bank account (page 213) to the trial balance on page 219.
- Transfer from the trial balance at 30 June 2001 (page 206) to the trial balance at 31 July 2001 the balances of the following accounts:

Vehicles

Office equipment

Stock

Bank loan

Capital

Drawings

- Total each column of the trial balance: the debit column and credit column should be the same.

11 As you have recently joined Sunny Days the office manager, Jane Jagpal, asks for your views on aspects of the accounts system and the way the accounts office is run. In particular, she mentions the following:

- With only yourself (full-time) and Mike Venn (part-time) as accounts staff, the accounts office is often empty at various times of the day, eg lunch time, and at morning and afternoon breaks.
- The computer used for payroll is often left switched on all day.
- The petty cash box is kept on top of a desk with the key either in the box or hanging from a hook close by.
- Double-entry accounting records are kept out on the desk all the time.
- Trial balances are kept in the filing cabinet, but the key to the cabinet has been lost and the drawers are kept unlocked.

Write a note to Jane Jagpal highlighting the problems and suggesting improvements.

Use page 220 for your answer.

ANSWER PAGES

Task 1

TRIAL BALANCE OF SUNNY DAYS AS AT 30 JUNE 2001

	Debit	Credit
	£	£
Name of account		
Purchases	....	....
Sales	....	....
Purchases returns	....	....
Sales returns	....	....
Discount allowed	....	....
Discount received	....	....
Wages	....	....
Rent paid	....	....
Rates	....	....
Bank charges	....	....
Postages	....	....
Stationery	....	....
Travel	....	....
Bad debts written off	....	....
Sundry expenses	....	....
Vehicles	....	....
Office equipment	....	....
Stock	....	....
Cash control	....	....
Bank	....	....
Debtors control	....	....
Creditors control	....	....
Value Added Tax	....	....
Inland Revenue	....	....
Bank loan	....	....
Capital	....	....
Drawings	....	....
	....	....

Tasks 2 – 8 and 10

MAIN (GENERAL) LEDGER

Purchases

Date	*Details*	*Amount* £	*Date*	*Details*	*Amount* £

Sales returns

Date	*Details*	*Amount* £	*Date*	*Details*	*Amount* £

Purchases returns

Date	*Details*	*Amount* £	*Date*	*Details*	*Amount* £

Sales returns

Date	*Details*	*Amount* £	*Date*	*Details*	*Amount* £

Tasks 2 – 8 and 10 continued

MAIN (GENERAL) LEDGER

Discount allowed

Date	*Details*	*Amount* £	*Date*	*Details*	*Amount* £

Discount received

Date	*Details*	*Amount* £	*Date*	*Details*	*Amount* £

Wages

Date	*Details*	*Amount* £	*Date*	*Details*	*Amount* £

Rent paid

Date	*Details*	*Amount* £	*Date*	*Details*	*Amount* £

Tasks 2 – 8 and 10 continued

MAIN (GENERAL) LEDGER

Rates

Date	*Details*	*Amount* £	*Date*	*Details*	*Amount* £

Bank charges

Date	*Details*	*Amount* £	*Date*	*Details*	*Amount* £

Postages

Date	*Details*	*Amount* £	*Date*	*Details*	*Amount* £

Stationery

Date	*Details*	*Amount* £	*Date*	*Details*	*Amount* £

Tasks 2 – 8 and 10 continued

MAIN (GENERAL) LEDGER

Travel

Date	Details	Amount £	Date	Details	Amount £

Bad debts written off

Date	Details	Amount £	Date	Details	Amount £

Sundry expenses

Date	Details	Amount £	Date	Details	Amount £

Cash control

Date	Details	Amount £	Date	Details	Amount £

Tasks 2 – 8 and 10 continued

MAIN (GENERAL) LEDGER

Debtors

Date	*Details*	*Amount* £	*Date*	*Details*	*Amount* £

Creditors control

Date	*Details*	*Amount* £	*Date*	*Details*	*Amount* £

Value Added Tax

Date	*Details*	*Amount* £	*Date*	*Details*	*Amount* £

Inland Revenue

Date	*Details*	*Amount* £	*Date*	*Details*	*Amount* £

Task 3

Petty Cash Book										PCB 47
Receipts	Date	Details	Voucher No	Total Payment	Analysis columns					
					VAT	Postages	Stationery	Travel	Sundry	
£	2001			£	£	£	£	£	£	
100.00	1 Jul	Balance b/d								
	5 Jul	Taxi fare	78	5.46	0.81			4.65		
	9 Jul	Stationery	79	9.40	1.40		8.00			
	12 Jul	Postages	80	4.30		4.30				
	17 Jul	Donation	81	5.00					5.00	
	20 Jul	Rail fare	82	8.09				8.09		
	24 Jul	Stationery	83	7.05	1.05		6.00			
	27 Jul	Postages	84	6.70		6.70				
	31 Jul	Taxi fare	85	5.00	0.74			4.26		

Task 4

SCHEDULE OF STANDING ORDERS AND DIRECT DEBITS

Date due	Details	Amount	Authorised by
5th each month, from August 2001 to July 2004	Wyvern National Bank – loan account repayments	£625	Jane Jagpal
17th each month, from January 2001 until further notice	Astra Property Rental – rent paid on business premises	£1,450	Jane Jagpal
18th each month, from April 2001 to March 2002 inclusive	Wyvern Council – rates	£696	Jane Jagpal

SCHEDULE OF BANK GIRO CREDITS

Date due	Details	Amount	Authorised by
20th each month, from April 2001 until further notice	Tyax Country Stores – debtor	£2,000	Jane Jagpal
28th each month, from September 2001 until further notice	Garden Time Limited – debtor	£1,500	Jane Jagpal

Task 4 continued

WYVERN NATIONAL BANK PLC

PO Box 301, Broad Street, Wyvern WY1 2DB

Account: Sunny Days
Account no: 80423621
Date: 30 July 2001

STATEMENT OF ACCOUNT

Date	Details	Payments	Receipts	Balance
2001		£	£	£
1 Jul	Balance b/d			14,976
3 Jul	Credit		12,747	27,723
5 Jul	Credit		8,932	36,655
9 Jul	Cheque No 101274	10,854		25,801
11 Jul	Credit		15,073	40,874
16 Jul	Cheque No 101276	10,347		30,527
16 Jul	Cheque No 101275	3,076		27,451
17 Jul	Direct debit: Astra Property Rental	1,450		26,001
18 Jul	Credit		3,096	29,097
19 Jul	BGC: Tyax Country Stores		2,000	31,097
20 Jul	Standing order: Wyvern Council	696		30,401
23 Jul	Cheque No 101277	4,863		25,538
27 Jul	Cheque No 101278	6,405		19,133
31 Jul	Cheque No 101280	11,292		7,841
31 Jul	Bank charges	55		7,786

CASH BOOK

Date	Details	Bank	Date	Details	Cheque number	Bank
2001		£	2001			£
1 Jul	Balance b/d	14,976	2 Jul	RP Industries	101274	10,854
3 Jul	Western DIY	12,747	6 Jul	Inland Revenue	101275	3,076
5 Jul	Raven Enterprises	8,932	10 Jul	Alpha Manufacturing	101276	10,347
11 Jul	Western DIY	15,073	16 Jul	Wyvern Wood	101277	4,863
18 Jul	Garden Time Ltd	3,096	20 Jul	Tritton Ltd	101278	6,405
31 Jul	Osborne plc	2,854	27 Jul	Dayton & Co	101279	2,741
			31 Jul	Wages	101280	11,292

Task 4 continued

REASONS WHY THE CASH BOOK BALANCE DIFFERS FROM THE BANK STATEMENT BALANCE

1. ....

2. ....

3. ....

Task 5

Details for reconciliation of the creditors control account

Purchases day book:

	Gross	VAT	Net
Totals for July 2001	£58,280	£8,680	£49,600

Purchases returns day book:

	Gross	VAT	Net
Totals for July 2001	£2,068	£308	£1,760

Discount received: total for month £307

Balances in subsidiary (purchases) ledger at 31 July 2001	£
Alpha Manufacturing	19,498
Dayton and Company	17,304
Eveshore Woodwork	8,794
RP Industries	22,153
Tritton Limited	18,743
Wyvern Wood	9,487

Reconciliation of creditors control account with subsidiary (purchases) ledger at 31 July 2001

	£	£
Closing balance of creditors control account		....
Balances of accounts in subsidiary (purchases) ledger:		
Alpha Manufacturing	....	
Dayton and Company	....	
Eveshore Woodwork	....	
RP Industries	....	
Tritton Limited	....	
Wyvern Wood	....	
Total		....
Imbalance (if any)		....

Task 7

Details for reconciliation of the debtors control account

Sales day book:

	Gross	VAT	Net
Totals for July 2001	£73,320	£10,920	£62,400

Sales returns day book:

	Gross	VAT	Net
Totals for July 2001	£2,632	£392	£2,240

Discount allowed: total for month £478

Balances in subsidiary (sales) ledger at 31 July 2001	£
C & R Garden Centres	35,090
Garden Time Limited	16,816
Osborne plc	12,893
Raven Enterprises	11,204
Tyax Country Stores	8,974
Western DIY	42,376

Reconciliation of debtors control account with subsidiary (sales) ledger at 31 July 2001

	£	£
Closing balance of debtors control account		....
Balances of accounts in subsidiary (sales) ledger:		
C & R Garden Centres	....	
Garden Time Limited	....	
Osborne plc	....	
Raven Enterprises	....	
Tyax Country Stores	....	
Western DIY	....	
Total		....
Imbalance (if any)		....

Task 7 continued

Note to Jane Jagpal, Office Manager

Task 8

COMPUTER SUMMARY

Payroll analysis for the month ended 31 July 2001

Gross pay	Income tax	Employees' NIC	Employer's NIC	Net pay
£16,284	£3,745	£1,247	£1,438	£11,292

Wages and salaries control account

Date	*Details*	*Amount* £	*Date*	*Details*	*Amount*

Task 9

STOCK RECORD

Product: plastic garden chairs — 'Relaxa' brand

Stock units: chairs

Date	Details	In	Out	Quantity in stock	Value at £20 per chair
2001					£
1 Jul	Opening balance			200	4,000
3 Jul	Receipt	100		300	6,000
5 Jul	Issued		30	270	5,400
6 Jul	Issued		20	250	5,000
9 Jul	Issued		50		
11 Jul	Issued		40		
13 Jul	Receipt	150			
16 Jul	Issued		36		
18 Jul	Issued		24		
19 Jul	Receipt	100			
20 Jul	Damaged		2		
24 Jul	Issued		28		
25 Jul	Issued		42		
27 Jul	Issued		38		
30 Jul	Receipt	150			
31 Jul	Issued		32		

RECONCILIATION OF STOCK TAKE AND STOCK RECORD AS AT 31 JULY 2001

	£
Physical stock take	....
Stock record card balance	....
Difference	....

Note to Jane Jagpal:

Task 10

TRIAL BALANCE OF SUNNY DAYS AS AT 31 JULY 2001

Name of account	*Debit* £	*Credit* £
Purchases	....	....
Sales	....	....
Purchases returns	....	....
Sales returns	....	....
Discount allowed	....	....
Discount received	....	....
Wages	....	....
Rent paid	....	....
Rates	....	....
Bank charges	....	....
Postages	....	....
Stationery	....	....
Travel	....	....
Bad debts written off	....	....
Sundry expenses	....	....
Vehicles	....	....
Office equipment	....	....
Stock	....	....
Cash control	....	....
Bank	....	....
Debtors control	....	....
Creditors control	....	....
Value Added Tax	....	....
Inland Revenue	....	....
Bank loan	....	....
Capital	....	....
Drawings	....	....
	....	....

Task 11

Note to Jane Jagpal, Office Manager

Unit 4 Practice Simulation

Flour Pot Bakery

suggested time 3 hours

SCENARIO

This Simulation is based on Flour Pot Bakery, a business which operates from four shops in the Wyvern area and produces bread, pastries, speciality cakes and 'take-away' snacks. The tasks in the simulation involve providing financial information and reports to management. They include:

- the coding of sales figures, suppliers' invoices and payroll data
- checking coding on invoices and identifying errors
- completing a performance report for cost centres and identifying discrepancies
- completing a performance report for sales and identifying discrepancies
- dealing with queries which involve confidentiality and referral to higher authority

NVQ UNIT 4 – ELEMENTS COVERED

1 code and extract information

2 provide comparisons on costs and income

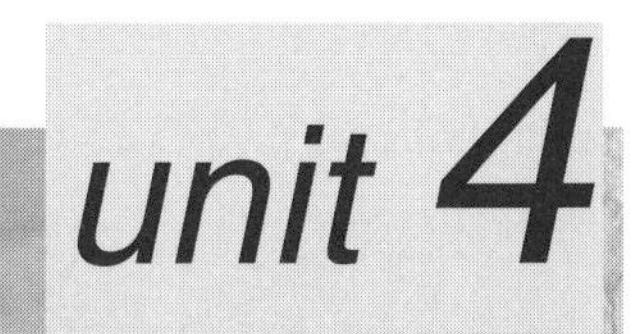

PRACTICE SIMULATION FLOUR POT BAKERY

SITUATION

You are Alex Wright, an Accounts Assistant at the main office of Flour Pot Bakery Limited, at 61 Fore Street, Wyvern WV1 3GH. The company is VAT registered.

The business operates at four locations:

- the main office and production facility at Wyvern – these premises also include a shop counter
- three shops in the nearby towns of Appleford, Great Marcle and Norton

Flour Pot Bakery has three types of product, all of which are produced at Wyvern:

- bread and 'everyday' cakes such as doughnuts, rock cakes, pastries and cream cakes
- 'take-away' film-wrapped and packaged rolls, sandwiches and filled baguettes, mainly for lunchtime customers
- speciality personalised iced cakes made to order, eg wedding cakes, birthday cakes, anniversary cakes

Your work as an Accounts Assistant involves supplying accounting information for the management of the business. This includes:

- coding income and expenditure from invoices and other documents
- extracting and presenting information for management as required

You report directly to Mike Moore, the Accounts Supervisor and are also helping to train a new assistant, Jade Simmons.

CODING SYSTEM

The six digit coding system used by Flour Pot Bakery is organised as follows:

coding of income

Example: 10 30 05

The first two digits are always 10, which shows that it is an *income item* (the code for costs is 20)

The second two digits show the *profit centre*:

10	Appleford
20	Great Marcle
30	Norton
40	Wyvern

The final two digits show the *type of product* which was sold:

05	bread and cakes
15	packaged 'take-away' snacks
25	speciality 'to order' cakes

coding of costs

Example: 20 30 05

The first two digits are always 20, which shows that it is an *cost item* (the code for income is 10)

The second two digits show the *cost centre* (which is always allocated to the Wyvern site):

50	baking
60	cake icing for speciality cakes
70	packaging
80	administration/shop costs
90	advertising

The final two digits show the *classification of cost:*

55	materials
65	labour
75	expenses

Examples of the coding system in use

Norton shop sales of bread	103005	= income (10) from Norton (30) from bread and cakes (05)
Wyvern shop sale of sandwiches	104015	= income (10) from Wyvern (40) from sandwiches (15)
Wages paid to bakery workers	205065	= a cost (20) from baking (30) related to labour (65)
Film used to wrap sandwiches	207055	= a cost (20) from packaging (70) materials (55)

TASKS

1 The date is 31 May 2001. You have in front of you the Daily Coding Sheet (page 225) which shows the income and expenditure against each code for the month to date.

There are a number of purchases invoices in your in-tray (pages 226 to 228) that need to be coded. For each of these you work out the appropriate code and write the number in the coding 'box' on the invoice. Mike Moore, the Accounts Supervisor, reminds you that the costs of the photocopier are to be shared equally between the administration and advertising departments.

After coding, you enter the money amounts of the invoices on the Daily Coding Sheet in the column for 31 May. Note that amounts are to be rounded to the nearest £; any VAT element of invoices is to be ignored – this is coded separately.

2 Towards the end of the day, on 31 May, the four shop managers e-mail (page 229) you with details of their sales (excluding any VAT element) for the day. You code this income and enter it on the Daily Coding Sheet (page 225). Remember to round amounts to the nearest £.

3 On 31 May the Staff Manager gives you payroll details for the week commencing 21 May of two employees who have recently joined the company. They are:

Ramjit Singh (baking department) – worked 40 hours on basic pay of £5 per hour, plus 4 hours of overtime at £7.50 per hour. There was no bonus or commission and the employer's National Insurance Contributions amounted to £17.81.

Daisy Chang (administration department) – worked 40 hours on basic pay of £5.50 per hour, but no overtime. There was no bonus or commission and the employer's National Insurance Contributions amounted to £16.59.

You are to enter these details on the schedules on page 230 to work out the labour cost to the business.

You are then to update the Daily Coding Sheet (page 225) with this data as it has not yet been entered. Remember to round amounts to the nearest £.

Note that the company's policy is to charge all payroll costs (including overtime and employer's National Insurance Contributions) to labour costs.

4 From the Daily Coding Sheet (page 225) you calculate the new balances for the month to date at the end of 31 May. These month-end figures are then taken to the summary of income and expenditure (page 231) and listed in the current month column.

On the summary of income and expenditure you complete the column for the year to 31 May 2001.

5 From the calculations performed in Task 4 you are to complete the Cost Performance Report for materials, labour and expenses on page 232.

6 Mike Moore, the Accounts Supervisor has asked you to examine the figures on the Cost Performance Report for materials, labour and expenses on page 232 and to calculate the cost discrepancies (variances) on the Report form on page 232. You are to identify any discrepancies (variances) of 10% or more and note them on the bottom of the form.

7 From the calculations performed in Task 4 you are to complete the Sales Performance Report for sales for the four shops on page 233.

8 Mike Moore, the Accounts Supervisor has also asked you to examine the figures on the Sales Performance Report for sales on page 233 and to calculate the discrepancies (variances) on the report form on page 233. You are again to identify any discrepancies (variances) of 10% or more and note them on the bottom of the form.

9 The date is 1 June 2001. You have been asked to check the coding on three supplier invoices received in the post today and processed by the trainee Jade Simmons (pages 234 to 235). Write down on the note (page 235) any errors you think you need to bring to her attention.

10 The date is 1 June 2001. While you are at lunch Jade takes a message (page 236) from the manager of the Norton shop who is asking for the sales figures for all the shops. The figures have been requested by a market research company. Write down (page 236) what you think you would tell Jade about the release of this information and the authorisation needed.

DAILY CODING SHEET: INCOME AND EXPENDITURE **Date:** 31 May 2001

MONTH TO: 30 MAY 2001

Note: figures are rounded to nearest £

Code No	Month to date (£)	Amounts for 31 May (£)	Month to date: new balance (£)
101005	25,076		
101015	30,164		
101025	4,024		
102005	15,958		
102015	10,844		
102025	4,091		
103005	22,032		
103015	13,197		
103025	6,478		
104005	31,070		
104015	35,264		
104025	17,406		
205055	51,287		
205065	42,753		
205075	20,264		
206055	6,833		
206065	9,170		
206075	6,182		
207055	5,437		
207065	10,551		
207075	8,327		
208055	3,596		
208065	12,504		
208075	6,652		
209055	4,076		
209065	10,387		
209075	3,932		

INVOICE

WYVERN MILLERS LIMITED

The Mill, Wyvern, WV4 1QT
VAT Reg 341 7821 27

CODE:

invoice to

Flour Pot Bakery Limited
61 Fore Street
Wyvern
WV1 3GH

invoice no 6281
account 3191
your reference 367
date/tax point 25 May 2001

product code	description	quantity	price	unit	total	discount	net
351	Stoneground baking flour	50	18.50	bag	925.00	0.00	925.00

goods total	925.00
VAT	0.00
TOTAL	925.00

terms
Net 30 days

INVOICE

Bakers Supplies Limited

47 Smith Street, London, EC3V 9AQ
VAT Reg 472 8391 82

CODE:

invoice to

Flour Pot Bakery Limited
61 Fore Street
Wyvern
WV1 3GH

invoice no 3741
account 2741
your reference 369
date/tax point 25 05 01

product code	description	quantity	price	unit	total	discount	net
861	Cake boxes, size 5	500	0.25	each	125.00	0.00	125.00

goods total	125.00
VAT	21.87
TOTAL	146.87

terms
Net 30 days

INVOICE

Wyvern Engineering Company

Brunel Road, Wyvern, WV3 8TA
VAT Reg 278 3524 91

CODE:

invoice to

Flour Pot Bakery Limited
61 Fore Street
Wyvern
WV1 3GH

invoice no 4071
account 0308
your reference 361
date/tax point 24 05 01

product code	description	quantity	price	unit	total	discount	net
001	Repairs to cake icing machine	1	155.00	each	155.00	0.00	155.00

goods total	155.00
VAT	27.12
TOTAL	182.12

terms
Net 30 days

CODE:

INVOICE

Severnvale Photocopiers Limited

Unit 40, Severn Business Park, Bridgetown, BG2 8QP
VAT Reg 396 0451 76

invoice to

Flour Pot Bakery Limited
61 Fore Street
Wyvern
WV1 3GH

invoice no 7046
account 0989
your reference 375
date/tax point 29 May 2001

product code	description	quantity	price	unit	total	discount	net
105	Service charge on Torriba photocopier	1	89.50	each	89.50	0.00	89.50

goods total	89.50
VAT	15.66
TOTAL	105.16

terms
Net 30 days

INVOICE

CODE:

Jarvis Advertising Services

48 East Street, Hollycombe, TU26 8LV
VAT Reg 981 3976 42

invoice to

Flour Pot Bakery Limited
61 Fore Street
Wyvern
WV1 3GH

invoice no 7842

account 0519

your reference 305

date/tax point 25 05 01

product code	description	quantity	price	unit	total	discount	net
HSB	Summer advertising promotion	1	785.00	each	785.00	0.00	785.00

goods total	785.00
VAT	137.37
TOTAL	922.37

terms
Net 30 days

INVOICE

Osborne Stationery Limited

Unit 5, Temeside Estate, Clifton Wells, CL4 7AP
VAT Reg 334 7921 45

CODE:

invoice to

Flour Pot Bakery Limited
61 Fore Street
Wyvern
WV1 3GH

invoice no 2073

account 3743

your reference 371

date/tax point 29 May 2001

product code	description	quantity	price	unit	total	discount	net
HT45	Box files, black	50	2.50	each	125.00	00.00	125.00

goods total	125.00
VAT	21.87
TOTAL	146.87

terms
Net 30 days

TEXT OF E-MAILS RECEIVED FROM THE FOUR SHOPS

To: Alex Wright, Accounts Assistant
From: Manager, Appleford
Date: 31 May 2001
Sales report: Appleford shop

Bread and cakes	£974.54
Packaged 'take-away' snacks	£1,386.68
Speciality cakes	£251.22

All figures are net of VAT, where appropriate.

To: Alex Wright, Accounts Assistant
From: Manager, Great Marcle
Date: 31 May 2001
Sales report: Great Marcle shop

Bread and cakes	£732.36
Packaged 'take-away' snacks	£401.49
Speciality cakes	£198.89

All figures are net of VAT, where appropriate.

To: Alex Wright, Accounts Assistant
From: Manager, Norton
Date: 31 May 2001
Sales report: Norton shop

Bread and cakes	£842.08
Packaged 'take-away' snacks	£508.76
Speciality cakes	£312.94

All figures are net of VAT, where appropriate.

To: Alex Wright, Accounts Assistant
From: Manager, Wyvern
Date: 31 May 2001
Sales report: Wyvern shop

Bread and cakes	£1,245.33
Packaged 'take-away' snacks	£1,348.60
Speciality cakes	£797.27

All figures are net of VAT, where appropriate.

PAYROLL COSTING SCHEDULE

Name	Payroll period	
Department		TOTAL (£)
Basic pay hours	Pay rate (per hour)	
Overtime hours	Pay rate (per hour)	
Bonus		
Commission		
Employer's NICs		
	TOTAL EMPLOYER COST	
	CODE	
	input by	date

PAYROLL COSTING SCHEDULE

Name	Payroll period	
Department		TOTAL (£)
Basic pay hours	Pay rate (per hour)	
Overtime hours	Pay rate (per hour)	
Bonus		
Commission		
Employer's NICs		
	TOTAL EMPLOYER COST	
	CODE	
	input by	date

SUMMARY: INCOME AND EXPENDITURE
YEAR ENDING 31 DECEMBER 2001

Code No	Description	Year to 30 Apr 2001 (£)	Current month: May 2001 (£)	Year to 31 May 2001 (£)
	INCOME			
	Bread and cakes			
101005	Appleford	123,049		
102005	Great Marcle	90,078		
103005	Norton	102,076		
104005	Wyvern	152,731		
	Packaged snacks			
101015	Appleford	161,421		
102015	Great Marcle	47,385		
103015	Norton	60,996		
104015	Wyvern	167,082		
	Speciality cakes			
101025	Appleford	35,025		
102025	Great Marcle	20,697		
103025	Norton	35,776		
104025	Wyvern	76,374		
	EXPENDITURE			
	Materials			
205055	Baking	247,291		
206055	Cake icing	29,843		
207055	Packaging	22,047		
208055	Administration/shop costs	12,976		
209055	Advertising	8,241		
	Labour			
205065	Baking	195,834		
206065	Cake icing	33,176		
207065	Packaging	42,958		
208065	Administration/shop costs	42,324		
209065	Advertising	29,722		
	Expenses			
205075	Baking	88,391		
206075	Cake icing	22,482		
207075	Packaging	30,056		
208075	Administration/shop costs	17,641		
209075	Advertising	35,024		

COST PERFORMANCE REPORT

May 2001

	Actual £ May 2001	Budget £ May 2001	Actual £ Year to date	Budget £ Year to date
MATERIALS		65,000		375,000
LABOUR		85,000		390,000
EXPENSES		47,000		250,000

COST DISCREPANCIES (VARIANCES) REPORT

May 2001

	MONTH £	YEAR TO DATE £
MATERIALS		
LABOUR		
EXPENSES		

COMMENTS

SALES PERFORMANCE REPORT

May 2001

	Actual £ May 2001	Budget £ May 2001	Actual £ Year to date	Budget £ Year to date
APPLEFORD		56,000		364,000
GREAT MARCLE		33,000		195,000
NORTON		40,000		235,000
WYVERN		90,000		540,000

SALES DISCREPANCIES (VARIANCES) REPORT

May 2001

	MONTH £	YEAR TO DATE £
APPLEFORD		
GREAT MARCLE		
NORTON		
WYVERN		

COMMENTS

INVOICE

JOHNSON PACKAGING LTD

6 Highfield Trading Estate Lampeter LL4 7YG
VAT Reg 235 6257 23

CODE: *20 50 65*

invoice to

Flour Pot Bakery Limited
61 Fore Street
Wyvern
WV1 3GH

invoice no	7724
account	246
your reference	377
date/tax point	25 05 01

product code	description	quantity	price	unit	total	discount	net
6667	Foodwrap film 750mm	100	4.50	roll	450.00	90.00	360.00

goods total	360.00
VAT	63.00
TOTAL	423.00

terms
Net 30 days

INVOICE

Wyvern Press

Windsor House, Hylton Road, Wyvern WV3 6BZ
VAT Reg 893 4572 12

CODE: *20 90 75*

invoice to

Flower Garden Designs
89 Fore Street
Wyvern
WV1 3GH

invoice no	2705
account	4226
your reference	390
date/tax point	24 05 01

product code	description	quantity	price	unit	total	discount	net
LP	Classified Advert	1	120.00	each	120.00	0.00	120.00

goods total	120.00
VAT	21.00
TOTAL	141.00

terms
Net 30 days

INVOICE

Confectionery Supplies Limited

29 Stockley Estate, Bristol, BS5 7FG
VAT Reg 462 3409 57

CODE: *20 60 55*

invoice to

Flour Pot Bakery Limited
61 Fore Street
Wyvern
WV1 3GH

invoice no 2721
account 5291
your reference 364
date/tax point 25 05 01

product code	description	quantity	price	unit	total	discount	net
FI67	Fondant icing ref67	10	12.00	packs	120.00	18.00	102.00

goods total	102.00
VAT	00.00
TOTAL	102.00

terms
Net 30 days

NOTE

to ______________________________

from ______________________________

date ______________________________

TELEPHONE MESSAGE

to Alex Wright

from Jade Simmons

date 1 June 2001 12.15

Emma Jones, Manager of the Norton shop 'phoned to say that a market research company was doing a survey of local shopping trends and wanted to know what the sales of our four shops were.
What should I tell her?
I said someone would phone her back this afternoon.
Thanks

Jade

what would you tell her?

Unit 3

Practice Central Assessment 1

Eveshore Engineering

It is recommended that students spend three hours completing the tasks, allocating the time as follows:

Section 1	90 minutes
Section 2	90 minutes

PRACTICE CENTRAL ASSESSMENT 1 EVESHORE ENGINEERING

INTRODUCTION

This practice Central Assessment is in two sections:

- Section 1 Processing Exercise – complete all five tasks
- Section 2 Ten tasks/questions – complete all tasks/questions

You are advised to spend 90 minutes (1.5 hours) on Section 1 and 90 minutes (1.5 hours) on Section 2.

Sections 1 and 2 both relate to the business described below.

DATA

- Angie Vader is the owner of Eveshore Engineering, a business which manufactures engine and gearbox components for customers in the motor industry.
- You are employed by the business as a book-keeper.
- Double-entry takes place in the main (general) ledger and the individual accounts of debtors and creditors are kept in subsidiary ledgers as memorandum accounts.
- Today is 31 July 2001.

TRANSACTIONS

The following transactions all occurred on 31 July 2001 and have been entered into the relevant primary accounting records (given below). No entries have yet been made into the ledger system. VAT has been calculated at the rate of 17.5%.

PURCHASES DAY BOOK

Date 2001	*Details*	*Invoice No*	*Total £*	*VAT £*	*Net £*
31 July	Wyvern Metal Co	851	2,350	350	2,000
31 July	Engineering Supplies Ltd	342	2,820	420	2,400
31 July	Osborne Limited	978	3,055	455	2,600
31 July	Tyax Services	101	3,525	525	3,000
	Totals		11,750	1,750	10,000

PURCHASES RETURNS DAY BOOK

Date 2001	*Details*	*Credit Note No*	*Total £*	*VAT £*	*Net £*
31 July	Osborne Limited	CN 41	282	42	240
31 July	Engineering Supplies Ltd	CN 85	423	63	360
	Totals		705	105	600

CASH BOOK

Date 2001	*Details*	*Discount Allowed*	*Bank £*	*Date 2001*	*Details*	*Discount Received*	*Bank £*
31 July	Balance b/d		6,200	31 July	Rates paid		650
31 July	Rent received		200	31 July	Tyax Services	50	1,950
31 July	Loan: BVB Bank		5,000	31 July	Wyvern Metal Co		1,000
				31 July	Balance c/d		7,800
			11,400			50	11,400

BALANCES TO BE INSERTED IN LEDGER ACCOUNTS

The following balances are relevant to you at the start of the day on 31 July 2001:

	£
Creditors:	
Engineering Supplies Limited	1,960
Osborne Limited	750
Tyax Services	2,500
Wyvern Metal Company	1,200
Purchases	276,147
Purchases returns	3,240
Creditors control	44,395
Discount received	840
Rent received	1,400
Rates paid	990
Loan: BVB Bank	2,500
VAT (credit balance)	7,330

Balances to be transferred to trial balance

	£
Premises	150,000
Machinery	55,000
Vehicles	44,000
Stock	28,270
Cash control	100
Debtors control	90,240
Capital	200,000
Sales	495,231
Sales returns	6,838
Discount allowed	1,080
Wages and salaries	84,514
Electricity	3,660
Telephone	2,175
Miscellaneous expenses	5,722

SECTION 1: PROCESSING EXERCISE

Task 1.1 Enter the opening balances listed on the previous page (239) into the following accounts which are provided on the next three pages (241, 242 and 243):

Engineering Supplies Limited
Osborne Limited
Tyax Services
Wyvern Metal Company
Purchases
Purchases returns
Creditors control
Discount received
Rent received
Rates paid
Loan: BVB Bank
VAT

Task 1.2 From the day books and cash book shown on pages 238 and 239 make the relevant entries into the accounts in the subsidiary (purchases) ledger and the main (general) ledger.

Task 1.3 Balance off all of the accounts showing clearly the balances carried down.

Task 1.4 Transfer the balances calculated in task 1.3, and from the cash book, to the relevant columns of the trial balance shown on page 244.

Task 1.5 Transfer the remaining balances shown above to the trial balance and total each column. The debit column and credit column totals should be the same.

Task 1.1, 1.2 and 1.3

SUBSIDIARY (PURCHASES) LEDGER

Engineering Supplies Limited

Date	*Details*	*Amount* £	*Date*	*Details*	*Amount* £

Osborne Limited

Date	*Details*	*Amount* £	*Date*	*Details*	*Amount* £

Tyax Services

Date	*Details*	*Amount* £	*Date*	*Details*	*Amount* £

Wyvern Metal Company

Date	*Details*	*Amount* £	*Date*	*Details*	*Amount* £

Task 1.1, 1.2 and 1.3 continued

MAIN (GENERAL) LEDGER

Purchases

Date	Details	Amount £	Date	Details	Amount £

Purchases Returns

Date	Details	Amount £	Date	Details	Amount £

Creditors Control

Date	Details	Amount £	Date	Details	Amount £

Discount Received

Date	Details	Amount £	Date	Details	Amount £

Task 1.1, 1.2 and 1.3 continued

MAIN (GENERAL) LEDGER

Rent received

Date	Details	Amount £	Date	Details	Amount £

Rates paid

Date	Details	Amount £	Date	Details	Amount £

Loan: BVB Bank

Date	Details	Amount £	Date	Details	Amount £

VAT

Date	Details	Amount £	Date	Details	Amount £

Task 1.4 and 1.5

TRIAL BALANCE AS AT 31 JULY 2001

	Debit	Credit
	£	£
Premises	....	....
Machinery	....	....
Vehicles	....	....
Stock	....	....
Bank	....	....
Cash	....	....
Debtors control	....	....
Capital	....	....
Sales	....	....
Sales returns	....	....
Discount allowed	....	....
Wages and salaries	....	....
Electricity	....	....
Telephone	....	....
Miscellaneous expenses	....	....
Purchases	....	....
Purchases returns	....	....
Creditors control	....	....
Discount received	....	....
Rent received	....	....
Rates paid	....	....
Loan: BVB Bank	....	....
VAT	....	....
TOTAL		

SECTION 2: TASKS/QUESTIONS

ANSWER ALL OF THE FOLLOWING TEN TASKS/QUESTIONS

- Suggested time allocation: 90 minutes (1.5 hours)
- Write in the space provided

Important note: none of the details in Section 2 affect the transactions in Section 1.

2.1 The debtors control account of Eveshore Engineering has a debit balance of £90,240 as at 31 July 2001. Confirm the accuracy of this figure by completing the document below, using the following information:

	£
Balance of debtors control account as at 1 July 2001	78,069
Sales invoices issued in July	85,217
Sales credit notes issued in July	1,124
Receipts from debtors in July	71,462
Discount allowed in July	110
Bad debts written off in July	350

DEBTORS CONTROL ACCOUNT CHECK AS AT 31 JULY 2001

	£	£
Balance as at 1 July 2001		....
Sales invoices issued	....	
Sales credit notes issued	....	
Receipts from debtors	....	
Discount allowed	....	
Bad debts written off	....	
		....
Balance as at 31 July 2001		

2.2 Angie Vader, the owner of Eveshore Engineering, says to you: "I am pleased to see that the trial balance has balanced at 31 July; however, I have heard that there are still some book-keeping errors that may not be shown by the trial balance."

Name FOUR errors not shown by a trial balance:

....

....

....

....

2.3 The petty cash book of Eveshore Engineering for the week ending 27 July 2001 is shown below. Angie Vader asks you to total the analysis columns, restore the imprest amount to £100, and then balance the petty cash book and bring down the balance on 28 July 2001.

Note: none of the details below is relevant to Section 1.

Petty Cash Book									**PCB 35**
Receipts	Date	Details	Voucher No	Total Payment	Analysis columns				
					VAT	Postages	Stationery	Travel	Sundry
£	2001			£					
100.00	21 Jul	Balance b/d							
	23 Jul	Taxi fare	65	5.00	0.74			4.26	
	23 Jul	Stationery	66	4.70	0.70		4.00		
	24 Jul	Postages	67	2.25	-	2.25			
	25 Jul	Cleaning materials	68	7.05	1.05				6.00
	26 Jul	Taxi fare	69	4.00	0.59			3.41	
	26 Jul	Postages	70	2.85	-	2.85			
	27 Jul	Stationery	71	3.76	0.56		3.20		
	27 Jul	Donation	72	5.00	-				5.00
		Totals		34.61	3.64	5.10	7.20	7.67	11.00
34.61	31/7	Cash Rec'd.							
	31/7	Balance c/d		100					
134.61				134.61					
100.00	31/7	Balance b/d.							

2.4 When checking the items on the bank statement against the items in the cash book, some differences need to be written in the cash book to bring it up-to-date, while others are timing differences that should correct themselves by appearing on later bank statements.

Indicate with a tick which type of difference are the following:

	update the cash book	*timing difference*
• bank charges shown on the bank statement	....	....
• cheque drawn, not yet recorded on the bank statement	....	....
• direct debit for a business expense, shown on the bank statement	....	....
• amount paid into the bank, not yet recorded on the bank statement	....	....
• bank giro credit from a debtor, shown on the bank statement	....	....

2.5 Eveshore Engineering has an account, in the name of Universal Sales, that appears in the subsidiary ledgers for both debtors and creditors. Universal Sales is both a supplier to Eveshore Engineering and also a customer. The balances of the accounts of Universal Sales in the two subsidiary ledgers are:

	£
• debtors ledger	600 debit
• creditors ledger	400 credit

Angie Vader thinks that it would be a good idea to be able to set-off one account balance against the other – subject, of course, to the agreement of Universal Sales. Explain the book-keeping entries you would make in the subsidiary ledgers and control accounts to record the set off.

Subsidiary ledgers

Debit .... £..........................

Credit .... £..........................

Control accounts

Debit .... £..........................

Credit .... £..........................

2.6 Eveshore Engineering uses a computer program for its wages and salaries calculations. The totals of the payroll for July 2001 taken from the computer summary are:

	£
gross pay	12,470
net pay	8,991
income tax	1,872
employees' National Insurance Contributions	982
employer's National Insurance Contributions	1,145
employees' pension contributions	625

Note: none of the details above is relevant to Section 1.

Complete the wages and salaries control account, below, with the figures from the July payroll (date the transactions 31 July 2001).

Wages and Salaries Control Account

Date	*Details*	*Amount* £	*Date*	*Details*	*Amount* £

2.7 Complete journal entries for the following transactions (date the entries 31 July 2001):

(a) Eveshore Engineering buys a new machine for use in the factory. The cost is £1,200 + VAT and the machine is bought on credit from Norton Supplies Limited.

(b) Angie Vader instructs you to write off as a bad debt the account of Wyvern Systems, a business which has ceased trading. The amount of the debtor balance is £141, including VAT, and Angie tells you that VAT-relief is available.

(c) Angie Vader has taken some goods from the business for her own use. The amount of the goods is £200 + VAT.

Notes:

- *Narratives are not required.*
- *You are not required to make any adjustments to the accounts in Section 1.*

Date	Details	Debit	Credit
		£	£

2.8 If a trial balance fails to balance, list five steps which you would take in order to locate the error(s).

1. ....

2. ....

3. ....

4. ....

5. ....

2.9 The trial balance of Eveshore Engineering fails to balance; it is £200 less on the debit side than on the credit side. The errors are not found quickly and Angie Vader tells you to transfer the amount to a suspense account (see below).

A detailed examination of the book-keeping system locates the following errors on 3 August 2001:

- an electricity bill of £300 + VAT was paid by cheque but no entry was recorded in the electricity account (note: the correct entry was made in the VAT account)
- purchases account is overcast by £100

Complete the journal entries required to correct the above errors (narratives are not required) and show the book-keeping entries in suspense account.

Note: You are not required to make any adjustments to the accounts in Section 1.

Date	Details	Debit	Credit
		£	£

Suspense Account

Date	*Details*	*Amount*	*Date*	*Details*	*Amount*
2001		£	2001		£
31 Jul	Trial balance difference	200			

2.10 Eveshore Engineering buys in completed sets of gears from a specialist manufacturer. The gears are then assembled by Eveshore into completed gearboxes which are sold to customers in the motor industry. Today, a physical stock take of the sets of gears (code G 540) showed there were 482 sets in stock, at a cost of £20 each, giving a stock valuation of £9,640.

Angie Vader gives you the stock record card (below) and asks you to complete it and to make a reconciliation with the physical stock take. If there is an imbalance, make a note to Angie suggesting where you think the difference may have occurred.

STOCK RECORD

Product: gears – G 540

Stock units: sets of gears

Date	Details	In	Out	Quantity in stock	Value at £20 per set
2001					£
1 Jul	Opening balance			300	6,000
3 Jul	Receipt	100		400	8,000
5 Jul	Issued		30	370	7,400
6 Jul	Issued		20	350	7,000
9 Jul	Issued		25		
11 Jul	Issued		40		
13 Jul	Receipt	150			
16 Jul	Issued		35		
18 Jul	Issued		24		
19 Jul	Receipt	100			
20 Jul	Damaged		2		
24 Jul	Issued		28		
25 Jul	Issued		42		
27 Jul	Issued		37		
30 Jul	Receipt	150			
31 Jul	Issued		37		

RECONCILIATION OF STOCK TAKE AND STOCK RECORD AS AT 31 JULY 2001

Physical stock take £....................

Stock record card balance £....................

Difference £....................

Note to Angie Vader:

Unit 3

Practice Central Assessment 2

Paperstop

This sample Central Assessment is reproduced by kind permission of AAT.

It is recommended that students spend three hours completing the tasks, allocating the time as follows:

Section 1	90 minutes
Section 2	90 minutes

PRACTICE CENTRAL ASSESSMENT 2
PAPERSTOP

INTRODUCTION

This practice central assessment is in two sections:

- Section 1 Processing Exercise – complete all five tasks
- Section 2 Ten tasks/questions – complete all tasks/questions

You are advised to spend 90 minutes (1.5 hours) on Section 1 and 90 minutes (1.5 hours) on Section 2.

Sections 1 and 2 both relate to the company described below.

DATA

- Amy McInnes is the owner of a business which supplies office stationery, office equipment and printed brochures.
- The business name is Paperstop.
- You are employed by the company as a book-keeper.
- Double entry takes place in the main (general) ledger and the individual accounts of the debtors and creditors are therefore regarded as memoranda accounts.
- Today is 31 May 2000.

Transactions

The following transactions all occurred on 31 May 2000 and have been entered into the relevant books of prime entry (given below). No entries have yet been made into the ledger system. VAT has been calculated at the rate of 17 ½%.

SALES DAY BOOK

Date 2000	*Details*	*Invoice* No.	*Total* £	*VAT* £	*Net* £
31 May	HTP Limited	756	1,175	175	1,000
31 May	B Avery & Company	757	1,880	280	1,600
31 May	Garners Limited	758	1,645	245	1,400
31 May	Rowley & Rudge	759	2,350	350	2,000
	Totals		7,050	1,050	6,000

SALES RETURNS DAY BOOK

Date 2000	*Details*	*Credit Note No.*	*Total £*	*VAT £*	*Net £*
31 May	HTP Limited	CR18	235	35	200
31 May	Rowley & Rudge	CR19	141	21	120
	Totals		376	56	320

CASH BOOK

Date 2000	*Details*	*Discount Allowed*	*Bank £*	*Date 2000*	*Details*	*Discount Received*	*Bank*
31 May	Balance b/f		3,600	31 May	Motor Tax		90
31 May	B Avery & Company	100	3,900	31 May	Charitable donation		50
31 May	Rowley & Rudge		1,000	31 May	Bank charges		156
				31 May	Balance c/d		8,204
		100	8,500				8,500

Balances to be inserted in ledger accounts

The following balances are relevant to you at the start of the day on 31 May 2000:

	£
Credit customers	
HTP Limited	8,300
B Avery & Company	4,400
Garners Limited	1,850
Rudge & Rowley	4,700
Sales	225,185
Sales returns	1,080
Debtors control	63,816
Bank charges	100
Discounts allowed	700
Motor tax and insurance	180
VAT (credit balance)	11,198

Balances to be transferred to trial balance

Motor vehicles	28,300
Office equipment	7,000
Stock	35,587
Cash	75
Creditors control	34,880
Capital	16,723
Purchases	101,857
Purchases returns	366
Discounts received	132
Wages	37,843
Rent and rates	4,000
Electricity	814
Telephone	922
Motor fuel	780
Miscellaneous expenses	1,830

SECTION 1: PROCESSING EXERCISE

(Suggested time allocation: 90 minutes)

Task 1.1 Enter the opening balances listed on page 253 into the following accounts which are provided on pages 255, 256 and 257:

- HTP Limited
- B Avery & Company
- Garners Limited
- Rowley & Rudge
- Sales
- Sales returns
- Debtors control
- Bank charges
- Discounts allowed
- Motor tax insurance
- VAT

Task 1.2 From the day books and cash book shown on pages 252 and 253 make the relevant entries into the accounts in the subsidiary (sales) ledger and the main (general) ledger.

Task 1.3 Balance off all of the accounts showing clearly the balances carried down.

Task 1.4 Transfer the balances calculated in task 1.3, and from the cash book, to the relevant columns of the trial balance shown on page 258.

Task 1.5 Transfer the remaining balances shown on page 253 to the trial balance and total each column. The debit column and credit column totals should be the same.

Task 1.1, 1.2 and 1.3

SUBSIDIARY (SALES) LEDGER

HTP Limited

Date	Details	Amount £	Date	Details	Amount £

B Avery & Company

Date	Details	Amount £	Date	Details	Amount £

Garners Limited

Date	Details	Amount £	Date	Details	Amount £

Rowley & Rudge

Date	Details	Amount £	Date	Details	Amount £

Task 1.1, 1.2 and 1.3, continued

MAIN (GENERAL) LEDGER

Sales

Date	Details	Amount £	Date	Details	Amount £

Sales returns

Date	Details	Amount £	Date	Details	Amount £

Debtors control

Date	Details	Amount £	Date	Details	Amount £

Bank charges

Date	Details	Amount £	Date	Details	Amount £

Task 1.1, 1.2 and 1.3, continued

MAIN (GENERAL) LEDGER

Discounts allowed

Date	Details	Amount £	Date	Details	Amount £

Motor tax and insurance

Date	Details	Amount £	Date	Details	Amount £

Charitable donations

Date	Details	Amount £	Date	Details	Amount £

VAT

Date	Details	Amount £	Date	Details	Amount £

TRIAL BALANCE AS AT 31 MAY 2000

	Debit £	Credit £
Motor vehicle	……..	……..
Office equipment	……..	……..
Stock	……..	……..
Bank	……..	……..
Cash	……..	……..
Debtors control	……..	……..
Creditors control	……..	……..
VAT	……..	……..
Capital	……..	……..
Sales	……..	……..
Sales returns	……..	……..
Purchases	……..	……..
Purchases returns	……..	……..
Bank charges	……..	……..
Discounts allowed	……..	……..
Discounts received	……..	……..
Wages	……..	……..
Rent and rates	……..	……..
Electricity	……..	……..
Telephone	……..	……..
Motor tax and insurance	……..	……..
Motor fuel	……..	……..
Charitable donations	……..	……..
Miscellaneous expenses	……..	……..
Total		

SECTION 2: TASKS/QUESTIONS

ANSWER ALL OF THE FOLLOWING TEN TASKS/QUESTIONS

- Suggested time allocation: 90 minutes (1.5 hours)
- Write in the space provided or circle the correct answer. Do not indicate your choice in any other way.

2.1 Complete the paying-in slip below to bank the cash that Paperstop has in its safe today:

One	**£20 note**	**Four**	**50p coins**
Three	**£10 notes**	**Ten**	**20p coins**
Three	**£ 5 notes**	**Twelve**	**10p coins**
Four	**£ 1 coins**	**Forty**	**2p coins**

Date ____________

Cashier's stamp and initials

bank giro credit

Code no	40 23 88
Bank	HSBC Bank PLC
Branch	Haglowen

Credit Paperstop

Account No. 31176786

Number of cheques

Paid in by ____________

Do not write below this line

£50 notes		
£20 notes		
£10 notes		
£5 notes		
£2/£1		
50p		
20p		
10p,5p		
Bronze		
Total Cash		
Cheques etc		
£		

2.2 Paperstop is considering using an analysed sales day book and sales returns day book. **Suggest THREE ways in which Paperstop may wish to analyse its sales.**

....

....

....

....

2.3 **Name THREE items of capital expenditure and THREE items of revenue expenditure that Paperstop is likely to incur.**

Capital expenditure	**Revenue expenditure**
....	....
....	....
....	....

2.4 Paperstop operates a monthly payroll system and all of the payroll figures pass through a wages and salaries control account. **Name FOUR entries you would expect to see in the wages and salaries control account.**

....

....

....

....

2.5 **Complete the following sentences:**

a) Paperstop sends out a .... to inform the customer that its order has been received and is being dealt with.

b) Paperstop sends out an .... to inform the customer when the goods on order will be delivered.

c) Paperstop sends out a .... to request payment BEFORE goods are delivered.

d) Paperstop raises a .... to record the receipt of goods into its warehouse.

2.6 Paperstop has always filed its correspondence with customers and suppliers in date order, but as the business has grown this system is no longer effective. **Suggest ONE method of filing correspondence which would be more appropriate.**

....

....

2.7 The following errors and adjustments are to be corrected in Paperstop's accounting records:

a) an amount of £100.00 has been credited to the bank charges paid account instead of the bank interest received account;

b) an amount of £34.00 has been debited to the motor fuel account and the same amount credited to the bank account, instead of the correct figure of £43.00;

c) a credit customer, Gee & Company, has ceased trading and the amount outstanding on its account of £600 plus VAT is to be written off as a bad debt.

Complete the journal entries required to correct the above errors.
NB: You are NOT required to make any adjustments to the accounts in Section 1. No narratives are required.

Date	Details	Dr	Cr

2.8 The creditors control account has a credit balance of £34,880 as at 31 May 2000. **Confirm the accuracy of this figure by completing the document below using the following information:**

Balance of creditors control account as at 01 May 2000	**£ 37,612**
Purchase invoices received in May	**£ 5,413**
Purchase credit notes received in May	**£ 874**
Payments made in May	**£ 6,981**
Discounts received in May	**£ 290**

CREDITORS CONTROL ACCOUNT CHECK AS AT 31 MAY 2000

	£	£
Balance as at 01 May 2000		....
Purchases invoices received	....	
Purchases credit notes received	....	
Payments made	....	
Discounts received	....	....
		________
Balance as at 31 May 2000		________

2.9 **Give TWO reasons for maintaining a creditors control account.**

....

....

2.10 **Paperstop has received the following bank statement as at 30 May 2000 which you are to check against the cash book shown below.**

a) **Check the items on the bank statement against the items in the cash book and update the cash book accordingly. Total the cash book and clearly show the balance carried down.**
NB None of the details below are relevant to Section 1.

LOWLANDS BANK plc
15 George Street, Nottingham, NG11 8TU

To: Paperstop | **Account No 31176786** | **30 May 2000**

STATEMENT OF ACCOUNT

DATE	DETAILS	DEBIT	CREDIT	BALANCE
2000		£	£	£
1 May	Balance b/f			1,181
5 May	Cheque No 198470	100		1,081
5 May	Credit		480	1,561
8 May	Bank Giro Credit			
	Bakers Limited		3,000	4,561
10 May	Cheque No 198471	235		4,326
16 May	Direct Debit			
	Keen & Company	850		3,476
24 May	Bank charges	56		3,420
25 May	Direct Debit			
	Cox Cleaning	150		3,270
30 May	Cheque No 198473	80		3,190

D = Debit C = Credit

CASH BOOK

Date	**Details**	**Amount**	**Date**	**Details**	**Amount**
2000		**£**	**2000**		**£**
1 May	Balance b/f	1,181	1 May	Downing & Co	100
1 May	B King	480	5 May	GPT Limited	235
24 May	C West	8,000	12 May	H & L Insurers	6,821
25 May	L Kingsley	1,175	23 May	Conners Limited	80

b) Give THREE reasons why the balance in the cash book does not match the closing balance on the bank statement.

....

....

....

appendix

This appendix of photocopiable material comprises the following documents and layouts:

Dr | Cr

Date	Details	Amount	Date	Details	Amount
		£			£

Dr | Cr

Date	Details	Amount	Date	Details	Amount
		£			£

Dr | Cr

Date	Details	Amount	Date	Details	Amount
		£			£

JOURNAL

Date	Details	Folio	Dr	Cr

Date	Details	Folio	Dr	Cr

Date	Details	Folio	Dr	Cr

Sales Day Book

Date	Customer	Invoice No	Folio	Gross	VAT	Net
				£ p	£ p	£ p

Sales Returns Day Book

Date	Customer	Credit Note No	Folio	Gross	VAT	Net
				£ p	£ p	£ p

Purchases Day Book						
Date	Supplier	Invoice No	Folio	Gross	VAT	Net
				£ p	£ p	£ p

Purchases Returns Day Book						
Date	Supplier	Credit Note No	Folio	Gross	VAT	Net
				£ p	£ p	£ p

CASH BOOK

RECEIPTS | PAYMENTS

Date	Details	Discount allowed	VAT	Cash	Bank	Date	Details	Discount received	VAT	Cash	Bank
		£	£	£	£			£	£	£	£

PETTY CASH BOOK

Receipts	Date	Details	Voucher No.	Payment	Analysis columns				
					VAT				
£ p				£ p	£ p	£ p	£ p	£ p	£ p

download further financial documents from our website and find out about our full range of accounting books and resources

www.osbornebooks.co.uk

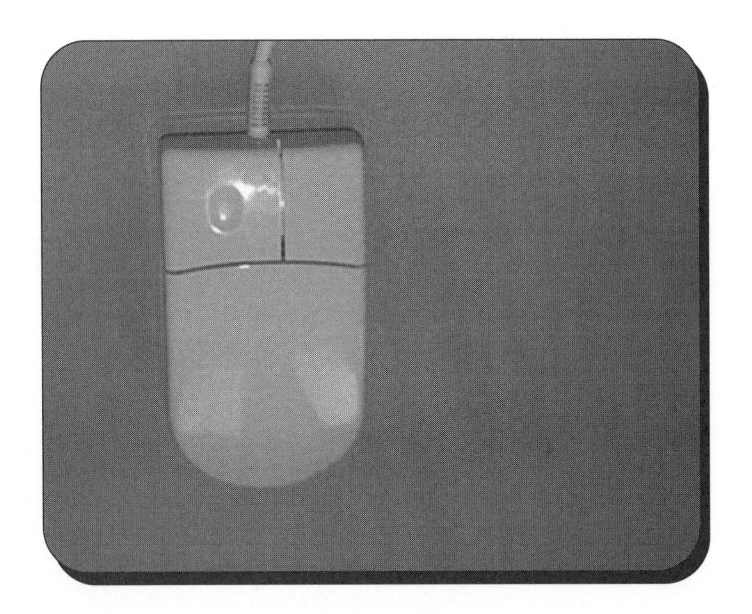